£1. 00

THE BOOK OF LIFE

Mebsadie D Dawkins

PUBLISHER'S NOTE

It is our vision to have *The Book of Life* widely distributed throughout the world. After reading it, refer to the back pages for information about how to obtain copies to share with interested friends and people who would appreciate your thoughtfulness.

With the publication of this first U.S. edition we are proceeding with arrangements to have English language editions published in other countries, as well as editions offered in German, French, Russian, Italian, Greek, Spanish, Hindi, Arabic, Japanese, Mandarin (Chinese), and other world languages. Publishers and their agents are invited to inquire.

THE
BOOK
OF
LIFE

Everyone's
Common Sense Guide
to Purposeful Living
& Spiritual Growth
into the 21st Century
and Beyond

Roy Eugene Davis

CSA PRESS, *Publishers*
CENTER FOR SPIRITUAL AWARENESS
Lakemont, Georgia 30552

ISBN 0-87707-234-5

CSA Press, *Publishers*
Post Office Box 7
Lakemont, Georgia 30552

CSA Press is the publishing department of
Center for Spiritual Awareness. Offices and
retreat center on Lake Rabun Road, Lakemont,
Georgia (U.S.A.) Telephone (706) 782-4723.

In West Africa:
Centre for Spiritual Awareness
Post Office Box 507, Accra, Ghana

Peter Oye Agencies, post Office box 5803
Lagos, Nigeria.

For addresses of distributors in other regions
of the world, contact the publisher.

PRINTED IN THE UNITED STATES OF AMERICA

Awakening From All Illusions

Because of increasingly influential evolutionary forces, our present era is one of accelerated transformations occurring in humankind's collective consciousness and dramatic changes in the world about us—and these processes will continue. The Dark Ages, the Time-Cycles of almost total, abysmal ignorance are behind us and new vistas, bright with promise, are before us for as far as our inner eyes can see.

If we are to thrive into the 21st century and beyond—and we must—heightened awareness, expanded knowledge, and skills more than equal to the needs and opportunities we will confront, are obviously necessary. Impractical ideas, illusional perceptions and thinking, and dysfunctional behaviors will have to be renounced: replaced by higher understanding, flawless powers of perception, and proficiency in the performance of duties and chosen actions. We can only successfully relate to the present and prepare for the future by awakening and actualizing our innate spiritual consciousness.

Except for the few saints and intellectual geniuses there are among us, we have yet to adequately awaken to a sufficient degree of realization of our essential being-ness. Our capacities to unfold knowledge and wisely use innate abilities are virtually limitless, yet we often as-

sume and behave just the opposite. The time has come for
us to accept a new paradigm, a more realistic, functional
point of view by which to relate to the world, and to
willingly and intentionally awaken to higher levels of
consciousness and function.

We need to know and live the Truth of ourselves: That
we are spiritual beings with only temporary identification
with mind and matter, not mere human beings with
perhaps hopeful aspirations for divine status. A radical
shift of perspective is necessary: from unknowing and in-
eptitude, to awareness of cosmic proportions and the unrestricted function and wisdom-guided expression it will
allow.

Philosopher-seers frequently remind us that our relationship with the physical universe is tenuous: not firmly
grounded because of Nature's insubstantial modes and
our own propensity for change. "Embodied life is always
uncertain," wrote Shankara of India fourteen hundred
years ago, "like a drop of water on a lotus leaf. The
company of saints and our own awakened spiritual consciousness can save and redeem us."

✓ No one else can do for us what we have the freedom and
ability to do for ourselves. Thankfully, we do have the
support and encouragement of enlightened souls, and we
do have God's grace. Grace is the enlivening, supportive
influence of the Spirit of God, all pervasive and expressive,
without which evolution could not continue nor we prevail
and grow. But knowledge we have, and grace, by which our
present and future good fortune is assured. ✓

I have had the blessing-opportunity to travel the world
and share these insights with hundreds of thousands of
men and women of many cultures and diverse circumstances. For more than four decades I have done this, and
whenever and wherever awakened consciousness has
allowed even partial understanding and impelled partici-

pation, I have seen worthwhile, sometimes even exceptional results.

✓Life itself is the "book" to be studied and its ways learned and adapted to practical, everyday relationships and endeavors. A timeless axiom reminds us that knowledge of consciousness is innate to consciousness. So it is consciousness, the reality-essence of ourselves and Nature, that we must explore if existing knowledge is to unfold in our awareness and blossom into wisdom. Then will all personal problems be spontaneously solved and will we have immediate, unrestricted access to the support of God and God's universe. ✓

✓We do not need to be persuaded to believe that we are immortal, spiritual beings predestined to awaken to transcendental levels of awareness, for our own intuitive knowledge of this fact is confirmation enough. But we do often need to be encouraged to come to terms with our spirituality, to learn to let it be expressive so that our lives demonstrate noble qualities and the fulfillment we desire and deserve can be actualized. ✓

The information shared here is for everyone. It will especially be appreciated by readers who are sincerely interested in purposeful living and committed to learning, understanding, and testing the principles described and recommended. For this, all that is required is right resolve and prudent exercise of common sense or inborn intelligence, a faculty every rational being has, and can with practice learn to effectively use.

As you proceed, set aside any preconceived notions you have. Endeavor to comprehend the words, as well as the states of consciousness which inspired them and the intention with which they were written. Whatever is not at first clearly understood, review until a reasonable degree of insight dawns in your awareness. But do not stop there, for knowledge is not empowering until personally applied and demonstrated to your complete satisfaction.

Every person, even the spiritually unawake, is impelled by an innate soul urge to become increasingly conscious and have awareness restored to its original, pure condition. This is the final consummation of our right actions and spontaneous spiritual unfoldments. We not only want to express in this world as free, functional beings; we desire above all to be liberated from illusions which are the basis of all troubles and limitations.

Whatever your present level of soul awareness or personal circumstances, may you now proceed to unfold your true potential and fulfill your soul destiny. This is my wish for you. You are an immortal, spiritual being with endless possibilities before you, known by God and knowable by you. Explore them with joy and thanksgiving.

Roy Eugene Davis

Lakemont, Georgia
Spring, 1993

Contents

Introduction:
Awakening From All Illusions   5

1. Where Are All the Saints?   11

2. What Do You Want?   19

3. What Everyone Should Know About
   the Reality, Being, Life, Power,
   and Substance of God   32

4. Progressing Through the Stages
   of Spiritual Growth   52

5. Meditation for Life Enhancement
   and Illumination of Consciousness   68

6. How to Pray: With Results Following   87

7. The Spiritual Basis of Real and
   Permanent Prosperity   100

8. The Usefulness of Healthy, Long
   Life with Enlightened Purpose   114

Appendix   144

1

Where are All the Saints?

There is a land of pure delight
Where saints immortal reign;
Infinite day excludes the night,
And pleasures banish pain.
Isaac Watts (1674-1748)

Hear my cry, O God; attend unto my
prayer. From the end of the earth will I cry
unto thee, when my heart is overwhelmed:
lead me to the rock that is higher than I.
The Book of Psalms 61: 1,2

When I was much younger, I wanted to tell the world
of the reality of God, save souls, and be instrumental in
helping heaven be fully manifest on Earth. I still do.

I think it not to be an idle dream that the best of which
is possible can be realized, expressed, and experienced by
us in our world. If what the saints say and what our hearts
inform us is true, and I'm sure it is, the universe includes
the fullness of God. It must then follow that the realm in
which we presently dwell is comprised of attributes and
qualities which provide for the unfoldment of virtually
endless possibilities.

Awakened spiritual consciousness enables us to more

easily understand, and participate with, the causative principles of the universe and its forces. And even before spiritual consciousness is fully actualized, our intentional endeavors to become more aware of life's processes and learn their actions facilitates spiritual growth to a remarkable degree. In ways which are often extraordinary in their outcomes, prudent use of common sense and sometimes even daring excursions into heretofore unexplored regions and fields of mind and matter, as healthy curiosity invites, can result in acquisition and unfoldment of knowledge and the spiritual fulfillment we yearn to actualize or demonstrate in fact.

That neither comprehensive understanding of our role in the universe, nor satisfying human happiness or real success in personal endeavors can be assured without a fair degree of awakened spiritual consciousness, has been believed and taught by philosophers and seers through the Ages. Regardless of our gender, nationality, cultural climate, profession or occupation, and whether religious or not, we need to expand our consciousness and grow spiritually in order to be healthy-minded, emotionally mature, and creatively functional. To deny this most basic need, upon which everything else we may consider to be worthwhile is based, is not only self-defeating but obscures the very purpose of our existence. Our lives can have no real meaning without comprehensive understanding and realized purpose. And these conditions cannot be present in a mind or consciousness which is closed to spiritual growth possibilities.

When I refer to spiritual growth I am not emphasizing traditional religious attitudes or relationships, although our religious opinions or practices may be instrumental in the spiritual growth process. I am referring to awakening to an awareness of the true essence, being, or Self of us, from which discovery we can proceed to explore the characteristics and operations of Nature as well as higher realities: the causative principles and active powers outside the range of ordinary sense perception and habitual thinking modes. To do this we need to desire spiritual growth, be willing to commit to it, and learn to exercise our innate intelligence, intuitive powers, and basic skills.

Our native intelligence, sometimes referred to as common sense, enables us to think rationally and accurately determine the validity of what is being analyzed. If intellect is dull, if mental and emotional confusion is allowed to prevail, thinking is muddled and frequent errors in judgment naturally result.

Intuition, our innate ability to know by knowing, the faculty of direct perception, enables us to have sudden insights which are not dependent upon experience, observed facts, or powers of reason alone. All subjective realities, when completely known, are apprehended intuitively. Sensory perceptions provide superficial knowledge of the environment, intellect provides more comprehensive knowledge, and intuition allows total realization.

Disciplined, skillful actions require concentration and definiteness of purpose. The more intelligently, skillfully purposeful we are, the more knowledgeable we can become. Conversely, the more ignorantly, skillfully purposeful we are, the more likely are we to further complicate our lives. My guru, Paramahansa Yogananda, used to occasionally comment about people he had known who were "very skillful in their ignorance!" Intelligent, skillful actions enable us to complete our purposes in life and fulfill soul destiny. Soul destiny is fulfilled when our awareness is fully restored to its original, pure condition.

Any intentional approach to living should successfully pass the tests of reason, intuition, and practical application. At the innermost depths of our being we should "know" the validity of the philosophical reasons for what we do. Our thoughts and actions should make sense when intellectually examined. Satisfying results will then follow. If we have adequate, relevant knowledge about how to proceed and act precisely in accord with it, we can be assured of desired outcomes. This holds true at every level of personal experience, including those which relate to psychological transformation and awakening of spiritual consciousness.

It is obviously only due to instinct, acquired behaviors, response to demands of challenging circumstances, and God's grace, that the majority of the citizens of Planet Earth function as well as they do. Over one half of them are barely surviving. A reasonable majority are coping to survive or demonstrating various degrees of material success. Only a few, perhaps ten percent of the total, are optimally functional and self-responsibly determining their personal affairs. Here and there, are a few truly spiritually conscious persons.

It's awesomely lonely in the universe without some degree of awakened spiritual consciousness, without the mental peace that knowledge of higher realities can provide and the assurance that only awareness of God's actual reality can allow. Many people do not even have the benefit of knowing that they are spiritual beings only temporarily relating to the human condition. They believe just the reverse: that thet are mere mortals, with perhaps some aspirations to divine status. Is it no wonder, then, that anxiety, fear, confusion, and admissions of purposelessness and hopelessness are so pervasive? And these symptoms are not confined to the Earth-realm or our present era; they are common to the soul condition wherever and whenever awakened spiritual consciousness is lacking.

Under the prevailing circumstances, we might reasonably think that multitudes of people would be beating at the doors of churches, temples, and various other institutions of learning, in a determined quest to further their spiritual and secular education! Or at least be sufficiently concerned about their present and future well-being to be motivated to more caring attention to their relationship with the universe. Instead, the tendency of the unenlightened mind is to pretend that almost everything is all right the way it is, that circumstances will work out by themselves, that the future will somehow take care of itself, and that death of the body only happens to other people.

This attitude of denial and avoidance is often carried over into the sphere of active religious or spiritual study and practice. The approach is frequently superficial, hard questions are seldom asked (or their honest answers appreciated), and participation is usually determined by personal convenience. The sometimes spoken, qualifying terms of involvement are: Don't tell me what to do. Leave my ego and weaknesses alone. I want to learn and benefit, if it's not too much trouble. And please don't stress the urgency of spiritual growth. Just give me the information and let me work things out in my own way, in my own good time.

To be decent about it, let's admit that everyone does indeed have the duration of Endless Time in which to spiritually awaken and fulfill soul destiny. At the risk of appearing discourteous, however, let's also be honest enough to admit to the obvious facts of the matter: that most people don't have the luxury of surplus time in their present incarnation to accomplish this. (There is an underlying cause of the problem of why otherwise reasonably rational people seem to prefer ignorance to knowledge and suffering to freedom. We will examine it and how to remove our awareness from its influences as we proceed through the following chapters.)

Using as an example a single Cosmic Person as an

analogy for collective human consciousness, the Cosmic Person is still sleeping but is beginning to become self-conscious—as during sleep, unconsciousness is usually dominant, with subconscious dream episodes occurring randomly. Now and then, consciousness hovers at the threshold of wakefulness and there are occasions of alert self-knowing. Sometimes, between the gaps, at the juncture-points between levels of awareness, there are flashes of insight and even incidents of transcendence during which the field of consciousness is absolutely clear and former states of consciousness are no longer influential—existing, if at all, as but faint memories.

This is how it is with us today. Unconsciousness and instinctive behavior are predominant in the human population. Most people who think of themselves as being conscious are really operating from a level of subconsciousness; with memories, emotional and sensory urges, and misperceptions being the ruling, determining factors in their experience. Now and then, there are interludes of partial awakening during which subconscious influences are seen in perspective and higher possibilities are momentarily glimpsed. Occasionally, and usually unexpectedly, undeniable certainty of self-existence is experienced and one feels capable of independent determination, with freedom to make choices. More rarely, but occurring with increasing frequency because of intentional, individual endeavor or spontaneous shifts of awareness, superconscious states and episodes of transcendental consciousness are experienced which allow access to knowledge corresponding to those levels.

Four factors are influential in the soul awakening process: 1) Our instinctive drives to survive in the face of challenge call forth our innate capacities to do so; 2) With a degree of self-consciousness, we begin to learn, exercise intelligence, and determine our personal circumstances—

we begin to grow; 3) The unalterable, insistent force of
evolution contributes to our spiritual growth because of
Life's urge to become increasingly conscious and expressive; 4) Enlivening and illuminating attributes of God in
Nature attract soul awareness to transcendent levels and
dissolve restricting characteristics which cloud consciousness and condition the mind, allowing the soul nature to
be Self-revealed.

The natural inclinations of evolution and the ordering,
enlivening, illuminating influences of higher consciousness result in life enhancing, supportive, inner transformations and outer adjustments of circumstances. These
are explained as evidence of God's grace because they are
not caused by our personal efforts, are unplanned by us
and are often unexpected. Grace, however, *can* be anticipated by us and our attitude of expectancy can enable us
to recognize and be responsive to its actions. Just as God's
grace is influential to the transformations which occur in
the universe and in collective and individual human
consciousness, so our own enlivened soul qualities and
capacities can contribute to our personal spiritual growth
experiences.

A seeker of truth asked his teacher, "Please, will you
pray that I receive an abundance of God's grace, and may
I have your blessings also?" To which the teacher replied,
"God's grace you already have, and my grace-blessing I
freely impart. Now all that is needed is your own grace."

Homo sapiens, humankind as we know it, has been on
Earth for at least 50,000 years (some anthropologists say
100,000 years or more, and oral traditions of some cultures
suggest a much longer duration). Except for the immediate past twelve centuries which comprise the extent of our
recorded history, very little is known with certainty. We do
know that much knowledge has been acquired, some of
which has been forgotten and is again coming to light, and

that new discoveries are being made with astonishing quickness. We have evidence before us that human consciousness is being transformed into ever higher orders of awareness. There have been illumined men and women in past Ages and there are many with us today.

Spiritually illumined people are variously referred to as seers, sages, spiritual masters, or saints. These are some of the words we may use when attempting to indicate what we perceive to be outer evidence of inner grace—or exceptional qualities we may describe as being of divine origin because they are different from the ones we usually associate with ordinary states of consciousness. Which brings us to the question which is sometimes asked: Where are all the saints?

It is not necessary for us to be saints before we can recognize them, because we can obviously discern qualities of refinement and holiness in people even though we ourselves have yet to become spiritually cultured and sanctified. I am sure there are many thousands of saints on Earth today, in spite of the fact that few of them seem to require public acknowledgement to do the work they feel is theirs to accomplish.

We need saints, of course. We need their radiance to bless planetary and collective consciousness. We need their good works and their usual wise counsel. And we need their example as a model for our own lives. Our hearts are stirred and, even, thrilled when we are made aware of the existence of noble-minded, completely selfless men and women who seem to us to be grounded in peace of soul which can only be the result of their open relationship with God. We are certain they represent the ideal toward which we all are moving. And, hopefully, we aspire to be like them.

2

What Do You Want?

You made us for yourself, Lord, and our
hearts are restless till they rest in You.
Bishop Augustine (4th century)

Let patience have her perfect work, that
you may be perfect and entire, wanting nothing.
If any of you lack wisdom, let him ask of God.
The General Epistle of James 1: 1,2

If we listen very carefully, we can *hear* the universe
speaking to us. "What is it you really want?" it asks. Then
it whispers, "If you will but choose it, you can have it. But
be sure you really want it, for I will surely give it to you."

Our primary wants are few. 1) We want to have a
harmonious relationship with the universe, and thereby,
the support of Nature. 2) We want to have the resources
and means to satisfy our legitimate desires and fulfill
purposes. 3) We want to have peace of mind and be able to
enjoy life. 4) We want to awaken spiritually and have
awareness restored to its original, pure condition. These
entirely natural, acceptable desires are innate to the soul
and should be given priority over everything else. These
being fulfilled, our lives are complete. If neglected or

unfulfilled, our lives are impoverished.

Our habitual states of consciousness, mental attitudes, thoughts, emotional states, and behaviors should support our soul aspirations. This is what it means to follow our bliss: to choose modes of behavior and relationships which allow spiritual consciousness to blossom and soul satisfaction to be actualized.

Real fulfillment and true happiness cannot be experienced so long as we allow ourselves to be impelled by whims and sensory urges only, or by the choices made by a confused mind. In our hearts, we know this to be true.

The ideal is to choose and implement a lifestyle which is totally supportive of the fulfillment of our real needs, the actualization of our highest aspirations, and which will facilitate rapid spiritual growth and nurture it until fully actualized. To do this, review the second paragraph of this chapter and hereafter keep in mind the four primary wants of the soul which are grounded in our innate urge to realize wholeness and fulfillment.

Live with the understanding that you are a spiritual being, innately superior to your thoughts, emotional states, and environmental circumstances. Out of your awareness of who you are, your thoughts, emotional states, relationships, actions, and circumstances are determined. Knowing this, assume command of your life. You will then more easily function as a self-responsible being. Avoid illusional thinking which can cause you to falsely assume yourself to be a victim of circumstances over which you have little or no control.

Pay no heed to the self-defeating attitudes, behaviors, and circumstances which others whom you may know have chosen for reasons of their own. Love, bless, and wish them well, while avoiding sympathetic attitudes which might cause you to identify with their attitudes and behaviors. Decide for yourself that you will always choose to live without limitations.

Plan for eternity. Your relatively brief sojourn on Earth is but a parenthetical interlude in a much longer soul journey through space-time. Be realistic about fulfilling your worthy desires and major purposes in this life cycle, while knowing that you are not confined to it. Physical birthing and deathing are only incidents of temporary matter-identification and release, not the beginnings and endings of you. People with little or no awakened spiritual consciousness tend to cope with circumstances and perhaps plan for reasonably secure older age and death, or submerge their awareness in sensory enjoyments, frantically grasping at fleeting promises of superficial, uncertain human happiness. This is not for you if you are intent upon Self-discovery leading to completely conscious, functional freedom.

As you plan, when agreed upon a reasoned course of action, be committed to it. The way to the actualization of your desires is both straight and *strait*, at once direct and *exacting*. Clear, focused vision is required for absolute success, and nothing less should be considered or allowed to confuse your mind and disorganize your life. I am not recommending narrow-mindedness, but concentrated intention focused on major purposes. This will ensure that creative forces flow without interference from confused thought processes, unstable emotional states, or involvements and behaviors which are not relevant to actualizing spiritual growth.

Good intentions and inspired resolutions will be fruitful only if we remain committed to them. Weakened resolve, permitted distractions, procrastination, laziness, fear of success, and various forms of addiction can neutralize our resolve if allowed to be influential. Keep ever in mind that conviction of purpose and reasoned plans of action are essential to the success process in every aspect of living, including that of cultivating awakened spiritual consciousness.

Addictions are learned or acquired habits. It is not really the behavior or relationship that seems to be the problem. The cause is ego-fixation or self-centeredness, along with an attitude of dependency which results in feelings of helplessness. Thus self-confined by their attitudes, addictive personalities act out a life-script to confirm the illusional presumption of helplessness. What is needed to banish dependency attitudes and behaviors, is awareness of self-worth based on spiritual understanding. A more wholesome interest in living will then follow and divine qualities will be spontaneously expressed.

Thus soul-directed in purposeful endeavors, one has little or no inclination to allow self-defeating attitudes and behaviors to interfere with enjoyable, life enhancing activities and relationships. Symptoms of presumed helplessness are not only characteristic of people whose dysfunctional behaviors are obvious, they are also frequently dramatized by many in the mainstream of society who find it difficult to cope with challenges and changes which occur within and around them. Feeling themselves to be incapable of being in control of their own psychological states, or of outer circumstances, insecure people manifest a variety of neurotic behaviors and stress-related illnesses. Many clinical tests have determined that morbid mental and emotional states, and inability to manage stress, weaken the body's immune system, disturb normal function and lower resistance to disease.

It is a statistical fact that conditioned human consciousness is unstable and unreliable. Normal behaviors of groups of people confirm this to be so. Ninety percent of adult Americans, for instance, who work to earn money to provide for themselves, do not have a secure, regular savings and investment program to ensure their comfort and well-being after retirement. They will, instead, be dependent upon family, friends, or federal, state, or local government assistance in their later years. Approximately twenty percent of persons comprising sales organizations produce eighty percent of the business. Of members and participants of Protestant churches in the United States, 18 percent fund 80 percent of the annual budget. The majority of persons who implement a weight loss program will gain weight again a few weeks or months after completing the program. The average New Year's resolution is forgotten within the first two months. At least 75 percent of persons for whom a stress management program is prescribed, will neglect their routines once they have experienced a comfortable degree of relief. Two years of interested, focused involvement with spiritual practices, such as devotional reading, prayer and meditation, and attention given to "righteous" living, is the average duration of time that passes before the "devotee" becomes disinterested, preoccupied with secular matters, settles for being a believer of doctrine instead of a knower of Truth, or drifts into religious fantasy or fanaticism. At least ninety percent of those who invest time, energy and sometimes money, to learn how to facilitate spiritual growth, will drop out and return to their conditioned modes of behavior.

Two thousand years ago the author of the *Bhagavad Gita*, one of India's classic scriptures, has Sri Krishna, a central character in the book's theme, say: "Out of one thousand, one seeks the Truth; of those who seek, one here and there, perchance, realizes the Truth"—a one-in-a-million successful enlightenment quest, perhaps. And the human condition has not changed very much through the past two millennia.

It is not that we *cannot* accomplish our major purposes. *If we are not doing so, it is only because we have not chosen*

*them with definiteness of intention and followed through
with supportive actions.*

*If You Really Want to Live
with Intentional Purpose and
Experience Rapid Spiritual
Growth, Do These Things*

World scriptures declare it, saints affirm it, and in
your soul you know it—you are a spiritual being with
innate intelligence and exceptional capacities to flawlessly
live in harmony with the Creative Power that pervades
the universe. To be open to the full support of Nature, do
whatever is necessary to experience it. The very first thing
to do is to choose the highest and best of which is possible
for you. Speak the following words, with enthusiastic
conviction:

> *I want to experience and express awakened
> spiritual consciousness! I choose to have a harmo-
> nious relationship with the universe and the full
> support of Nature! I choose to thrive, to flourish,
> and be successful in every way! I choose to have
> peace of mind and enjoy life! I choose to awaken
> from all illusions and fulfill my spiritual destiny! I
> am committed to my choices and will do everything
> necessary to allow them to be fully realized!*

Regardless of existing personal circumstances, we
always have the freedom to choose to speak (to declare,
decree, or affirm) that which we desire to express in our
lives. When doing this, speak with clear intention and
settled conviction. Avoid moods or attitudes of hopeless
hope or vague wishfulness. Our conscious, intentional

speaking will:

* awaken soul awareness.
* clear and expand consciousness.
* order thoughts and mobilize energies.
* rearrange subconscious conditionings and harmonize emotional states.
* cause us to be fully aware in the present and removed from the effects of past causes.
* reinforce our commitment.
* inspire entirely constructive attitudes and actions.
* put us in tune with the creative forces of the universe.
* transmute our vital forces into more refined essences.
* beneficially influence brain and body chemistry.
* elevate us above mundane influences.
* attract to us whatever we desire and can accept.
* change forever the way we view our world.
* heal all troublesome conditions.
* enable the spontaneous actualization of soul capacities.

✓ When speaking like this we are not attempting to condition the subconscious level of our minds, nor endeavoring to modify our personality. If such changes are necessary, they will occur spontaneously. We are not demanding anything of the Higher Power. We are simply acknowledging the Truth: That we are spiritual beings agreeing to that of which we are entirely deserving. Therefore, do not speak indecisively, hoping for a few crumbs from the Cosmic Table. Speak the word and *be transformed by the renewing of your mind, then continue in that realized understanding.* ✓

Be prepared for changes in your life when you speak like this, because you are asking for them. You cannot be the newly awakened person you will be, and at the same time the old personality-person you formerly were. Whatever useful changes occur in your life as a result of your change in states of consciousness, welcome with gratitude. Do not yearn to cling to nonuseful behaviors, circumstances, and behaviors which will no longer be compatible with your elevated spiritual condition.

Give up the old ways and embrace the new ones. Let sad moods and self-defeating attitudes and behaviors be consigned to the past. They do not apply to you anymore. All power of heaven is ours but we often give it away by indulging in moods of self-pity and feelings of insecurity. Or we may whine and complain about circumstances, blame past events and other people, engage in gossip, and in similar ways poison our minds. Put an end to all destructive behaviors and influences by being settled in right understanding and courageous living. That is the way to proceed.

You are destined to fulfill your soul purposes. If it seems to you that you are not progressively experiencing their fulfillment, help yourself and let the universe help you by making constructive choices. Passive, fearful people sometimes say, "I'm afraid to make a decision because what I think I want may not be God's will for me." Or, "I'm always careful not to allow myself to have desires because I prefer to allow God's grace to operate in my life and reveal and unfold what is best for me." If your life is unfolding harmoniously, of course continue what you are presently doing. If it is not, choose what you consider to be the highest and best for yourself and for others with whom you share your life.

If we are sincerely committed to what is highest and best, we need not be concerned about whether or not our choices are compatible with God's will, for grace will always supersede when necessary, to make adjustments and ensure favorable outcomes. But if we are not willing to use our common sense and practical skills, including those which allow us to adjust states of consciousness and mental states, we have no one and nothing to fault but ourselves for any continuing frustration or discomfort. Unless one is mentally deficient or totally unconscious, there can be no excuse for failure to creatively use native intelligence and practical knowledge to improve circumstances. There may be faulty reasons but there are no acceptable excuses.

By the time you have finished a careful, comprehensive reading of this book you will know all you need to know about what to do after you have made intentional, constructive choices. If you spoke the words previously recommended, you have already entered into the processes of inner transformation and outer adjustments of circumstances. Now, it will be helpful to *write* your choices, to more accurately order your thoughts, share your aspirations with Universal Mind, and become increasingly open to all of the blessings of life you are capable of expressing and experiencing.

Before proceeding to the next chapter, pause. Be relaxed and calm, and respond to the guidelines and questions on the following pages. If you like, use a notebook or sheets of paper for this purpose. After you have completed the project, put what you have written in a private place for future reference. Be sure to write with clear intention and soul conviction. As you do this, feel yourself to be in tune with God and in harmony with universal forces.

My Choices for Having a Harmonious Relationship
with the Universe and the Support of Nature

Year, month, and day of these choices: _____

Affirmation:
I consciously choose to have a harmonious relationship
with the universe and the full support of Nature.

1. What conditions will prevail in your life when this
   choice is fully actualized or realized in fact?

   _____

   _____

   _____

   _____

   _____

2. With your present understanding, what do you honestly think you can do (and what are you willing to do)
   to allow yourself to have a harmonious relationship
   with the universe and the full support of Nature?

   _____

   _____

   _____

My Choices for Having the Resources and Means to Satisfy Desires and Fulfill Purposes

Year, month, and day of these choices: _____

Affirmation:
I choose to have abundant resources and available means to satisfy my legitimate desires and fulfill purposes.

1. What conditions will prevail in your life when this choice is fully actualized or realized in fact?

   _____

   _____

   _____

   _____

   _____

2. With your present understanding, what do you honestly think you can do (and what are you willing to do) to allow yourself to have abundant resources to satisfy your desires and to have your purposes fulfilled?

   _____

   _____

   _____

My Choices to Have Peace of Mind and to Be Able to Enjoy Life

Year, month, and day of these choices: _____

Affirmation:
I choose to have peace of mind and to enjoy life.

1. What conditions will prevail in your life when this choice is fully actualized or realized in fact?

    _____

    _____

    _____

    _____

    _____

2. With your present understanding, what do you honestly think you can do (and what are you willing to do) to allow yourself to have peace of mind and enjoy life?

    _____

    _____

    _____

    _____

My Choices for Realizing and Expressing Awakened Spiritual Consciousness

Year, month, and day of these choices: _____

Affirmation:
I choose with all my heart to realize and express awakened spiritual consciousness.

1. What conditions will prevail in your life when this choice is fully actualized or realized in fact?

_____

_____

_____

_____

_____

2. With your present understanding, what do you honestly think you can do (and what are you willing to do) to allow yourself to grow spiritually and to have your awareness restored to its original, pure condition?

_____

_____

_____

3

What Everyone Should Know About the Reality, Being, Life, Power and Substance of God

The infinite God, the great one life,
than whom is no other—only shadows, lovely
shadows of Him.
George MacDonald

In one verse I shall tell you what has been
taught in thousands of volumes: Brahman is
real, the world is false; the Self is
Brahman and nothing else.
Adi (the first) Shankaracharya

The fundamental need of every person is to know God as God is, and to fully, consciously realize the reality of God. Nothing else can satisfy the yearning of the heart's sincere desire.

This, being consummated, results in complete fulfillment. It also quite naturally results in the spontaneous ordering of our personal affairs and the solving of all problems formerly common to ordinary human experience. The outer expressions of inward grace, however, are incidental to it and are not the primary focus of our spiritually resolved endeavors.

We need not be advanced students of metaphysics to be aware of an obvious fact of the human condition: that as pleasant and satisfying as reasonably conscious, functional living can be, in the midst of even comfortable circumstances there yet remains within us a holy desire for a more permanent condition.

Our spiritual journey, being subjective or inward, defies comparison with our usual external relationships and experiences. It is entirely a matter of progressive soul growth—or, sometimes, sudden adjustments in attitude and states of consciousness—by which we awaken from prior states (and, therefore, from former ways of seeing and understanding things and circumstances) to levels more real and infinitely more mind and consciousness liberating. Expanded consciousness enables us to know and experience "the great one life" and to accurately perceive manifest expressions of it as "only shadows, lovely shadows of Him." Such perceptions calm the mind, satisfy the heart (the true Self of us) and provide assurance that we are, at last, fulfilling our innate urge to realize transcendental states of consciousness.

"God is real, the world is false!", proclaim the saints. But what do they mean by this statement? Do they mean that our world, whether presumed as lovely or judged to be a troublesome place, does not exist? No, this is not what is implied. The world does exist as a play of cosmic forces and is thus perceived and experienced. But it is not fixed in space and time; it is not permanent because it is ever changing. It had a beginning, an emergence into manifestation, and it will have an ending when it is eventually withdrawn into the formless, primal field of Nature-essence from which it emerged billions of solar years ago. Between cycles of objective world manifestation, the field of Primal Nature remains undisturbed, but with potential to again manifest universal processes.

The world, while it exists, is false in that it is but an outer appearance of a subjective, permanent reality. This is why seers teach that the world can be enjoyed but that attachments to it are to be avoided if peace of mind and spiritual awareness are to be maintained. Blind attachment to, or overdependence upon that which by its very character is impermanent, results in grief when the objects of attachment or dependence are removed by the inexorable transformations common to transitory circumstances. However, we cannot reject the world or refuse to have a relationship with it, because our present circumstances require that we dwell in it. What are we to do?

The recommended way to relate to the world is for us to play our roles in the light of understanding, while remaining focused on the ideal of facilitating awakened spiritual consciousness. In fact, if we are to remain healthy-minded and functional, this is all we can do. To become depressed or apathetic, or to more compulsively be involved with sensory relationships in a vain attempt to ignore our spiritual needs, is to perpetuate a condition of "living death"—a veiling of awareness which results in experienced degrees of unconsciousness.

Some people do not easily grow to emotional maturity. They instead cling to attitudes and behaviors more suitable to earlier stages of life and are referred to as being dysfunctional because of their arrested emotional condition. Too, many who are reasonably emotionally mature and functional are in a phase of arrested spiritual growth. They have matured to a stage of personality integration and functional competence but have neglected the cultivation of their spiritual capacities. For this reason they are unhappy in the midst of otherwise satisfactory circumstances. When they allow themselves to be self-honest, or when their soul nature cries out for expression, they are confronted by the disturbing truth that their human sufficiency is not entirely adequate. Nor can it be, for our lives are not our own—they belong to That which is the Higher Self of us, to God.

✓ A common obstacle to knowing God is disinterest. We might offer any number of seemingly reasonable arguments to refute this: lack of intelligence, a deficiency of knowledge about how to implement spiritual growth, psychological unrest, addictive behaviors, dysfunction because of trauma or stress resulting from the strain of daily living, and many competing interests and circumstances. But such contentions are not the result of reasoned conclusions; they are mere opinions based on incomplete understanding. They cannot stand in the light of knowledge about how goals are achieved and desired purposes are fulfilled. For when sufficient interest awakens curiosity and inspires enthusiasm to learn and to grow, our innate abilities and creative forces quite obviously become directed toward the acquisition of suitable knowledge which can enable us to fulfill purposes. More, when we help ourselves, Something larger than we are provides us with resources out of the fullness of Itself. ✓

✓ The word *God* has Sanskrit language origins and comes through Germanic and Old English languages. An ancestor word *hu* is found in the *Rig Veda*, the oldest known religious book of which we have present knowledge. It is used in reference to "the one who is invoked," whose influences are invited into human affairs by prayer and other means. But *what* or *who* is God? ✓

✓ According to philosopher-seers and saints, God is apprehended as the single manifesting Reality-aspect of pure Existence-Consciousness, often referred to as Supreme Consciousness, the Transcendental Field, or the Absolute. How God comes into expression and how the universes (and we) emerge from the field of God into the arena of space-time can be known by us.

Many earnest seekers of Truth embark upon a spiritual discovery path with little useful knowledge about how to proceed. Others, erroneously assuming themselves to be more capable, often attempt to actualize higher knowledge and experience by adapting it to their still conditioned mental states and states of consciousness. But just as fresh food can be contaminated if stored in an unclean container, so partially awakened spiritual consciousness can become spoiled when adulterated or mixed with delusions and illusions which may be present in the seeker's mind and consciousness. Some, blessed with holy desire, keen powers of intellect, willingness to learn and to apply what is learned, and surrendered humility, experience rapid spiritual growth and satisfy the soul's sincere desire to realize God in a relatively short duration of time.

Four basic, interdependent themes are at the core of this philosophical thesis and should be known, examined, and comprehended by anyone wishing to proceed to further study and practice for the purpose of facilitating psychological transformation and spiritual growth.

1. The universal laws of causation which relate us to the cosmos and contribute to our personal involvement with it. By knowing these, we can proceed to further examine the matter before us.

2. The universal processes which produce and maintain the cosmos, and provide the field of Nature in which life expresses. When unconsciously identified with these processes, souls relate to them almost exclusively, forgetful and unaware of higher realities and uncertain about the nature of God.

3. The field of absolute, nonmodified, pure consciousness or Supreme Consciousness. It is the substratum, the underlying support of the cosmos, making possible its

existence and vital operations. Realization of Supreme Consciousness is the consummation of our spiritual growth endeavors and unfoldments.

4. The practical means of experiencing liberation of consciousness. Grounded in philosophical understanding and knowledgeable in procedures which can facilitate spiritual growth, absolute soul freedom can be realized.

When allowed to be influential, our innate urge to have awareness restored to purity assures progressive spiritual growth. Our divine nature, the true Self of us, expands awareness to reclaim omnipresence. Assisted by Nature's evolutionary inclinations and the attracting, positive polarity of God, supportive forces assist us and are acknowledged as active expressions of God's grace. Once committed to learning and experience which practice can provide, it is not difficult to acquire higher knowledge and become God-realized. The important factor is our choice to awaken to our full potential. Choosing the higher way results in surrendered commitment. Surrendered commitment is the way of discipleship, and discipleship leads to enlightenment—full comprehension of the reality of God and liberation of consciousness.

Diverse are the ways devotees approach God, and various are their stations in life and their modes of action. Yet the universe is vast and there is a perfect place for everyone. It matters not what your past has been or what your present circumstances might be. The important matter is right resolve and dedicated endeavor. At the inmost center of your being you are already grounded in God. You now live in God. Knowledge and realization of God will surely be unfolded and actualized as you remain faithful to your high calling.

God and Universal Manifestation:
How the Cosmic Drama Unfolds

An ancient Vedic scripture proclaims: "That Existence which is without beginning or end, is Supreme Consciousness, the only real Substance." *Substance* here refers to that which is self-existent, complete within itself and having no prior cause. As such, it is *real* or permanent. Anything "unreal" is supported by that which is its cause for expression, and is therefore an appearance in space-time subject to modifications and changes. Supreme Consciousness forever exists and is the cause and support of all outer expressions in the field of Nature. It is by being grounded in awareness of Supreme Consciousness that we are able to remain unmoved while living in a world of transformation and change.

The most satisfying approach to understanding God is to examine higher realities in the light of reason and intuition, setting aside any preconceptions or prejudiced attitudes. In this way, unclouded intelligence will enable accurate determination of what is analyzed and intuition, our innate capacity to directly apprehend, will provide direct perception and insight. Unreasoned opinions, preconceptions, and compulsions to attempt to prove or defend immature philosophical views because of emotional insecurity, will obscure direct perception of what is true and result in further confusion rather than in clear understanding of the nature and operations of God.

What is here explained, when understood, will be seen as the underlying, revealed truth which supports all genuine religious experience and enlightened philosophical insights. Regardless of your past or present religious, philosophical, or scientific attitudes and experiences, an intellectual comprehension of this overview will prove helpful. It is only seldom that the entire range of universal processes are clearly comprehended upon an initial exposure to these ways of looking at God and the universe. What is more usual is that frequent, repeated examination is required, to allow time for adjustments in states of consciousness to occur and changes in attitude to transpire. Also, it is helpful to adapt what is learned to our everyday routines and relationships in order to test our knowledge and experience the life-transforming differences that only participation can provide. Knowledge is not our own until it has been tested and proved in the light of personal application. What is true, will stand; what is not true has no reliable foundation.

> In the beginning God created the heaven and the earth. And the earth was without form, and void; and darkness was upon the face of the deep. And God said, Let there be light: and there was light.
> *The First Book of Moses Called Genesis 1:1-3*

> In the beginning was the Word, and the Word was with God, and the Word was God. All things were made by him: and without him was not any thing made that was made.
> *The Gospel According to Saint John 1:1-3*

Since the Absolute, Supreme Consciousness, is outside of the field of space-time, it simply *is. Beginning,* in the scriptures, refers to the start of the emergence of the cosmos from the Godhead. God is the only expressed aspect of Supreme Consciousness, the only unfoldment from the field of pure Existence-Consciousness. Out of God the universes are expressed or manifested. Because world manifestation occurs because of an impulse to express rather than by an arbitrary act of will, seers say that God expresses because of motiveless necessity. Reason cannot be prior to manifestation because Universal or Cosmic

Sequence of Cosmic Manifestation

SUPREME CONSCIOUSNESS The Absolute field of pure Existence, outside of the field of space-time with potential to manifest.

MANIFESTING GOD CONSCIOUSNESS The Godhead, with attributes of Being, Power, and Intelligence.

FIELD OF PRIMAL NATURE Aum (Om), space, time, and cosmic forces and particles.

MANIFESTING COSMIC FORCES Expressing as luminosity, inertia, and the neutralizing influence.

COSMIC MIND Cosmic individualization and essence of individualized minds of souls.

ESSENCES OF ORGANS OF SENSES Of hearing, touch, sight, taste, and smell.

ESSENCES OF ORGANS OF ACTION Of speech, dexterity, mobility, reproduction, and excretion.

ESSENCES OF PRIMARY ELEMENTS Of ether,* air, fire, water, and earth.

Realms of Fine, Subtle and Gross Manifestation
    Of electrical properties (causal), life forces (astral), and physical universes, completing the processes of cosmic manifestation.

Ether, as used here, refers to the field of fine cosmic forces in space which are not-yet-matter but have the potential to manifest as matter.

Mind is also external to God and a product of universal manifestation.

It is helpful for us to remember that we are "made in the image and likeness of God," as specialized units of consciousness. Therefore, we are advised to endeavor to realize the truth of what we are and what God is, rather than attempt to attribute human characteristics to God. First by an exercise of imagination, then by experiencing a shift of viewpoint, endeavor to learn to see from God's point of view. An entirely different perspective will result, ridding the mind of illusory concepts about God and cosmic processes.

The *Word*, the creative force of God, literally produces the worlds out of itself. As a vibrational flow of current, it has a frequency and a discernible sound. We may attempt to approximate the sound of the creative current when we intone Aum or Om. The manifesting Word is evidence of the existence of That which is its origin, just as the universe is evidence of the existence of the single, creative force which produced it and makes all of its operations possible. Contemplatives who aspire to know and realize God often focus on the sound current, endeavor to be absorbed in it, and follow it to its source in God. This is extolled as a direct way to God-realization and is accessible to anyone who learns of the process and applies it.

As the Word flows into manifestation it becomes modified; appearing as space-time and fine cosmic particles. The four components of Primal Matter, then, are: the creative current, space, time, and cosmic particles. This field makes possible further expressions of all aspects of the cosmos and the varied forms of Nature. The field of Primal Nature has two fundamental characteristics: it is form-producing and Truth-veiling. Its form-producing characteristic gives birth to the worlds, which is why some devotees refer to God *as* Primal Nature as Divine Mother or Mother God. Its Truth-veiling characteristic obscures awareness and knowledge of souls involved with it. This is why souls identified with subtle matter become deluded: they are relating to "the darkness" of Primal Nature.

✓ As the result of such involvement, souls experience a veiling of intuition and a clouding of the faculty of intelligence. With the veiling of intuition, souls lose awareness of their essential nature: they become forgetful of God. With the clouding of intelligence, errors in perception result, which is why seers say that man's problems are due to the illusions which arise because of misperception. Awakening from illusions and from delusion can occur spontaneously as a radical adjustment of states of consciousness, or progressively as the result of flawless exercise of intelligence and intuition. Enlightenment, having awareness restored to complete Self-knowledge and God-realization, can be immediate or it can be developmental. It can be instantaneous or it can be slow, medium, or rapid, depending upon individual capacity and responsiveness to God's grace. ✓

If one is somewhat spiritually aware and almost prepared for sudden awakening, or is willing to fully surrender to transformation processes and spiritual growth episodes, enlightenment can occur quickly. If these conditions do not apply, one can enter into a program of intentional study and spiritual practice to facilitate psychological and spiritual growth. Progress is then determined by depth of holy desire, participation in spiritual practices and other wellness and growth enhancing processes, and God's grace. Even if a devotee is new on the spiritual path and the goal of enlightened God-knowledge seems far in the distance, that perception itself is illusory because every soul is ever grounded in the unbounded field of pure Existence-Consciousness which is the foundation reality of every soul and every thing. All that is needed is to learn how to comprehend this fact and realize it.

Three regulating attributes or qualities of consciousness pervade the field of Nature and have origins in the manifesting Word or creative current. One attribute is neutral, and from it, positive and negative polarity attributes are manifested. These attributes of the Word regulate cosmic forces. Without their influences, cosmic forces would exist as random and nondirected essences and universal manifestation would not be possible.

The neutralizing attribute is influential in all transformation processes. The positive polarity attribute contributes to brightness, lightness, and luminosity. The negative polarity attribute contributes to heaviness or inertia. These three characteristics are evident throughout the field of Nature and expressive in every manifest form, living things and creatures. When our minds are influenced by the neutralizing attribute we experience mental and emotional discontent or restlessness. We may have desires and feel the urge to satisfy them. We are impelled to action for one purpose or another. By regulating this attribute's influence upon us we can experience welcome inner changes and accomplish useful purposes.

When influenced by the positive polarity attribute we are inspired with noble thoughts and ideals; inclined to live in wholesome, constructive ways; to acquire higher knowledge; and to know God. These aspirations should be cultivated.

When influenced by the negative polarity attribute we tend to be lazy, sluggish, mentally dull. We may even be inclined to self-defeating behaviors and subject to moodiness and feelings of hopelessness and despair. These tendencies can be overcome by purposeful involvements so that we learn to live with high resolve and have entirely constructive purposes as directives in our lives.

Eventually, these influences are transcended and our

lives directed entirely by soul knowledge and divine impulses flowing from the field of God. Then, beyond the influences of relative causes, we live by enlightened choice and grace. In this way do we overcome the world even while continuing to participate with its processes. Nothing in the manifest universe then constrains us. Our lives effortlessly and spontaneously express soul qualities and capacities—the full, unrestricted powers of illumined consciousness.

The Spirit of God, the enlivening Life of God, shining on the field of Primal Nature, activates it and regulates its processes through the aforementioned three attributes and by Its innate Intelligence. God then becomes *imminent* (prominent, projecting, intruding) in the creation drama. This involvement results in the manifestation of Cosmic Individuality or Cosmic Soul. Reflected lights of the Spirit of God appear as specialized units of God consciousness, as individualized Selves of God, which is what we are. When seers recommend that we "search out the Truth in our hearts" they inspire us to Self-discovery through a process of subjective introspection. In this way we are able to discern that we are not bodies or minds— that we are spiritual beings, literally appearing in God's likeness. Just as the reality of God shines in the field of Nature and can be discerned, so our own reality shines in our mental field and can be clearly discerned. When it is, we are mentally illumined and functional as awakened spiritual beings.

As cosmic forces, regulated by the triple attributes of manifesting consciousness, flow into objective expressions with fine, subtle, and gross characteristics, the universe is produced and the characteristics of manifest Nature are determined by the influences and interactions of the three attributes. So, the universe has forever existence as Consciousness even though its beginning and endings in relative time-cycles are periodic. The universe was not created out of nothing: it was produced out of Primal Nature which, in turn, extends from the field of the Godhead.

As Cosmic Mindstuff or Universal Mind is manifested and Nature becomes specialized, individualized mental fields are produced from it to serve creatures and human beings. Fine cosmic forces which later manifest in more tangible form are produced by flows of cosmic forces to make possible the varied forms of Nature and bodies through which life can express.

Because of self-awareness the soul is conscious of itself as spirit. This is the seat of feeling or Self-apprehension. With this, a false sense of individuality arises, the ego-sense, which results in ego-fixation or blind self-centeredness. The egocentric soul, identified with fine cosmic matters and therefore devoid of higher knowledge, attracts to itself a mental field, a thinking and information processing medium comprised of the essences of Cosmic Mind. Another aspect of the mental field, which includes feeling, self-sense, and thinking skills, is the intellectual faculty which makes possible reasoned discernment. When mental processes are calm, intelligence can more easily be exercised. When mental processes are confused and emotions are unsettled, intellectual capacities are impaired. When the mental field is well-ordered or its operations stilled during meditation or moments of transcendence, the light of pure consciousness shines clearly in the intellectual aspect of the mind, illumining it.

The mind may be compared to a crystal which reflects that which is in proximity to it. When flooded with sensory impressions or mental activities, images and thoughts attract our attention and dominate consciousness. When the fluctuations and transformations of the mental field are calmed during meditation, the mind accurately re-

Cosmic Manifestation and Transformation of Radiant Forces

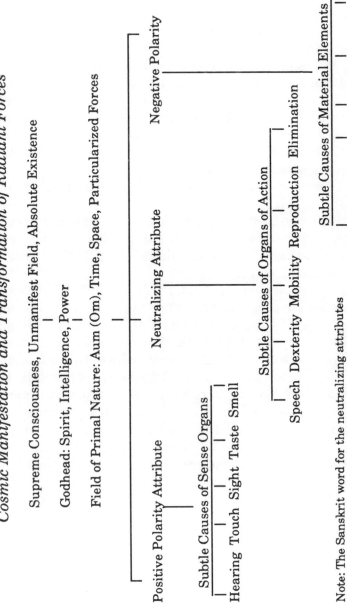

Supreme Consciousness, Unmanifest Field, Absolute Existence

Godhead: Spirit, Intelligence, Power

Field of Primal Nature: Aum (Om), Time, Space, Particularized Forces

Positive Polarity Attribute   Neutralizing Attribute   Negative Polarity

Subtle Causes of Sense Organs

Hearing   Touch   Sight   Taste   Smell

Subtle Causes of Organs of Action

Speech   Dexterity   Mobility   Reproduction   Elimination

Subtle Causes of Material Elements

Ether/Space   Air   Fire   Water   Earth

Note: The Sanskrit word for the neutralizing attributes is *guna*, that which binds and regulates flows of cosmic forces, causing transformations and changes.

flects the light of the soul.

The essences from which further subtle and gross manifestations on Nature are expressed comprise the *causal field*: it being the realm of causes which extend objective expressions of Nature. From the field of Cosmic Individualized Consciousness, under the influence of the outflowing surge of Spirit, five kinds of radiant force are projected from the three polarity attributes which regulate cosmic forces: one from the middle, two from the extremities, and two from each of the gaps or junctures between the three attributes (see chart).

The positive polarity characteristics of the five radiant forces or electricities are the essences of the five organs of perception—smell, taste, sight, touch, and hearing. These, being established in the mental field, make possible objective perceptions and serve as connecting links between inner and outer realms.

The neutralizing characteristics of the five radiant forces or electricities are the essences of the organs of action—excretion, generation, mobility, dexterity, and speech.

The negative polarity characteristics of the five radiant forces or electricities are the essences of the various sense objects in the field of Nature—ether or subtle matter-stuff in space, air, fire, water, and earth or gross particle manifestations.

The above fifteen attribute-essences comprise the fine sheath or body of the soul identified with subtle matter and persist when the soul is further identified with the astral or life force realms, and the physical realm.

The fifteen fine essences, plus the five gross material matter expressions, along with mental field characteristics of intellect, mind, feeling, and egoism, comprise the twenty-four categories of cosmic manifestation, with Supreme Consciousness being their cause and support, therefore, superior to them.

Some philosophers refer to the universe as God's cosmic body. God, being superior to the universe, and existing outside of its operations, is not contained by the universe although the universe is pervaded by God. Just as God is not limited by the cosmos, so we, as spiritual beings, are not limited by body or mind when we are enlightened. When ego boundaries are dissolved, the soul awakens to omnipresence and relates only to God. When even that relationship dissolves, transcendence is realized.

To the God-realized person the universe is apprehended as being expressive through fourteen spheres: seven manifest cosmic realms and seven vital places in the body of human beings. The seven cosmic realms are described below. The seven vital places in the body are described in the following chapter.

1. *The Realm of the Godhead.* God is the only real essence and substance involved in universal processes. Because the realm of the Godhead is beyond relative universal processes, it is referred to as *nameless* and *indescribable*. It can be known about by intellectual inquiry and intuitive analysis, and realized directly by an enlightened soul.

2. *The Realm of God's Spirit.* The field produced by the inclination of God's enlivening influence to manifest. It, too, is prior to relative cosmic processes but can be experienced during surrendered meditation and absorption of consciousness in the creative current or Word.

3. *The Realm of Spiritual Reflection.* At this level, specialized units of pure spirit originate. Religious literature describes it as the realm of the sons and daughters of God, the *devas* and *devis*, literally "the shining ones." As specialized units of consciousness they are also referred to

as the true Self and are God's light particularized.

4. *The Realm of Primal Matter.* The basic stuff of which the universe is comprised: creative force, space, time, and light particles. Referred to in the Christian scriptures as the *deep*, and the *waters* which are moved upon by the Spirit of God, resulting in motion, interactions, and further manifestation of itself as fine, subtle, and gross Nature. In Eastern scriptures it is referred to as maya, ("to measure"), which produces the forms of Nature and can veil the soul's powers of perception.

5. *The Realm of Magnetism and Aura-Electricities.* The causal realm of fine properties and essences with potential to further manifest in more obvious expression.

6. *The Realm of Electric Attributes.* Comprised of fine matters produced out of the preceding realm. The astral or life force realm. Souls flow through it to be born (identified with) in physical bodies and retire to it between Earth sojourns if they are still involved with cycles of reincarnation.

7. *The Realm of Gross Matter.* The physical realm experienced through the body's senses and comprised of the five element-influences: space (fine matters or cosmic forces); air (life force properties which move or circulate); fire (transformational forces); water (moistening, softening influences); earth (cosmic forces under the influence of inertia, particles). These objectify or manifest as what we presume to be material substance.

Within the last few decades of the 20th century it was discovered that what the ancient seers said is true: the material world is not at all what it appears to be to sense oriented perceptions. Instead of being inert substance, it is really a play of cosmic forces. Atoms, the building blocks of matter are comprised of units of energy which have their basis in what is referred to as a quantum field, where

actions and interactions occur which defy rational thinking. The universe we relate to is an electro-magnetic
phenomenon. The ordinary person's senses perceive perhaps but one billionth of the light spectrum. Discoveries
made in the fields of biology, cosmology, and physics have
so far revealed but a minute fraction of the totality of the
real nature and operations of the universe. For total
comprehension one will have to literally remove awareness from the senses and explore the subjective side of
Nature with heightened powers of intellect and unfettered
intuition. As soul awareness is relieved of the constric-
tions of delusion and illusional perceptions, all knowledge
of God and the universe can be spontaneously revealed.

The *Reality*, *Being*, *Life*, *Power*, and *Substance* of God
can almost completely be known by intellectual analysis
and entirely realized by direct perception and experience.
Only a person under the spell of illusions will assert that
God cannot be known, because his or her view of possibilities is obscured. Enlightened souls testify that they know
the Truth and their lives bear witness to their realization.

Our approach to higher knowledge and God-realization will depend upon our psychological temperament and
capacities, which is why there are different approaches to
actualizing awakened spiritual consciousness. All useful
approaches to God-realization culminate in enlightenment and liberation of consciousness. Discover your own
most successful way and honor the ways others are led to
their spiritual fulfillment.

Yearning, even burning, desire to realize God gives
rise to devotional ardor which can provide motive force to
keep us steady on our spiritual path. Such Holy desire
awakens our soul forces, purifies our thoughts and actions, and refines the body's nervous system so that higher
states of consciousness can operate. Also, since desire is
self-fulfilling, our Holy desire propels us to our desired

outcomes and attracts to us what we need in the way of knowledge and experience, so that we can learn and grow in understanding. Pure desire attracts divine influences into our lives so that spontaneous spiritual awakening occurs and grace becomes pronounced.

It is not necessary that you immediately understand all of the explanations given here, for you cannot possibly do so without awakened intuition. But an intellectual grasp of what is possible to comprehend will be helpful in enabling you to order your thoughts and behaviors, and can be a useful beginning on your inner journey to Self-realization and final enlightenment.

Reread this chapter frequently, knowing that the beingness of you already comprehends everything. As you apply your practical understanding to daily living and continue to awaken, all knowledge will be spontaneously revealed in your consciousness.

4

Progressing Through the Stages
of Spiritual Growth

Great works do not always lie in
our way, but every moment we may do
little ones excellently, that is,
with great love.
Saint Francis of Sales (1567-1622)

Every man has, and has had
from everlasting, his true and perfect
being in Divine Consciousness.
Alfred, Lord Tennyson (1809-1892)

Our powers of perception, psychological states, and
even our physiology, are influenced by our states of consciousness. Therefore, there are observable indications of
our spiritual growth which enable us to determine where
we are on the awakening path and what we can possibly
do to assist ourselves to continued or more rapid soul unfoldment.

Behind the facade of personality and body we are ever
the same as specialized units of pure consciousness, reflected lights of the Spirit of God. This should constantly
be remembered even while we are engaged in processes for

the purpose of improving function and facilitating spiritual growth. The ideal is for our increasing Self-realization, and the expanded states we experience, to be expressive through our minds and the physical body. As this occurs, our powers of perception improve, psychological states undergo orderly transformation, and the body's nervous system becomes more refined and capable of processing higher states of consciousness. It is occasionally possible to experience transcendent states of consciousness, only to lose awareness of them when returning to involvement with thinking, moods, body awareness, and everyday routines and relationships. We then have the memory of higher states of consciousness but are unable to experience them except during occasions of internal contemplation or those surprising moments of spontaneous elevation of consciousness. What is more desirable is to have higher states of consciousness persist during ordinary states of consciousness and everyday activities.

Seven broad categories, or levels, of soul awareness can be recognized. Each has psychological states, mental states, and behavioral tendencies common to them. Each can also be related to the seven vital centers in the human body because when our consciousness is identified with these centers our awareness corresponds to them.

The three states of consciousness experienced while in ordinary human consciousness are: unconsciousness, usually during deep sleep; subconsciousness, during dreaming sleep and moments of wakeful reverie; and the waking state during which we are usually self-conscious. There is often a blending of these states even when one is predominant. For instance, sometimes after awakening from deep, restful sleep, we have memory of how enjoyable it was to experience. There may also be occasions of lucid dreaming, during which time we are aware that we are dreaming. We may choose to allow the dream sequence to run its course, we may intrude upon it and change it somewhat, or we may decide to awaken from the dream. Finally, during our normal waking hours we may, simultaneously, be involved with memories, fantasy, or other subconscious influences. We have even had interludes of unawareness or unconsciousness during the waking state. We may suddenly experience mental blankness and have no awareness of ourselves or where we are.

While there can be occasions of spontaneous awakenings to much higher levels of awareness, it is more usual that we awaken from waking self-consciousness to superconsciousness, the fourth state; then to cosmic consciousness states, God conscious states, and transcendent states.

When firmly established in the fourth state we can be Self-realized; that is, we can consciously know ourselves as beings of pure consciousness, independent of mental operations, emotional states, and physical identification. We may continue to be aware of mental functions, feelings, and the body, but we remain as the objective witness of these conditions. This is a useful first awakening stage, from self-consciousness, because it enables us to independently choose our thoughts, moods, behaviors, and actions. From this level it is possible to beneficially influence physical functions and outer circumstances. This can be the first step in the direction of spiritual Self-mastery.

Preliminary superconscious states are usually mixed with mental influences and emotional states, even though they do allow experiences of deep calm and a degree of soul tranquility. As superconscious states are purified as a result of surrendered prayer and meditation, mental operations become naturally ordered, emotional states are harmonized, and undisturbed awareness of pure consciousness prevails. Repeated exposure of the mind and nervous system to episodes of pure consciousness purifies the mental field, refines the nervous system, and contributes to improved physical function.

Steady superconscious states provide the foundation for further subjective contemplation of higher realities and expanded states of consciousness. With expanded consciousness we are able to directly perceive and acknowledge our true relationship with the universe and know it for what it is: a manifestation of cosmic forces which have origins in the field of God. Thus we experience cosmic conscious states. Just as initial superconscious states may be mixed with influences common to the three normal states of human consciousness, so initial cosmic conscious states may likewise be influenced. Cosmic consciousness will then be partial until more awakening is experienced.

Just as not all human beings are alike in perceptual abilities and understanding, so not all superconscious persons are alike, nor are all cosmic conscious persons alike. There are characteristics which are common to ordinary human consciousness and characteristics which are common to categories of higher consciousness. Just as we do not expect every healthy-minded, functional human being to be a genius or to be without some character flaws, so we should not expect every superconscious or cosmic conscious person to be fully enlightened and infallible in their statements or actions. There are many Self-realized saints who are still working out psychological problems, involved in challenging personal circumstances, and who do not yet know everything there is to know about God and universal processes. They know the truth about themselves as spiritual beings but they are still contending with restricting characteristics of the mind or endeavoring to cleanse their consciousness of the "clouds of unknowing" which may still interfere with clear perception of the reality and allness of God.

Spiritual growth may be progressive or it may be erratic, depending upon our resolve and what we have to work out or overcome within ourselves. By choosing a total lifestyle which is supportive of spiritual growth, our progress is more likely to be steady. Even so, there may be interludes of challenge, of confusion, of what seems to be stagnation of growth. There may even be occasions of despair, when it seems that the future looks bleak and we feel somewhat hopeless. Should these incidents occur, remember: *Greatness of soul consists not only of our aspiration and ability to rise in consciousness, but also of our willingness to gather our spiritual forces and rise up again and again when we fall.*

Some conditions which can contribute to mental confusion and slowness of spiritual growth are: lack of aspiration, lack of devotion to God, laziness, irregular spiritual practice, association with purposeless or self-defeating behaviors of others, reading or exposing ourselves to spiritual teachings which are not truly inspired or valid, preoccupation with sensory experience, inattention to necessary details, and more. The most useful advice to follow is: find the way that is most result producing and persist in it. The important thing to remember is that your spiritual growth experiences are between you and God. You need not then be influenced by opinions of unenlightened people or do anything that will distract you from your high purpose.

Regardless of our outer circumstances, so long as they are orderly and life enhancing, your inner work and spiritual growth can proceed as a private endeavor. Except for persons who share your aspirations, no one need know about your inner practices or relationship with God. So do not say that you would do better if you had the support of others on the path. All outer support is valueless if we do not have our own support, and if we have this, we need not rely upon anything external, but only on God.

Spiritual growth can proceed regardless of your formal religious affiliation, or lack of it. You can continue your practices within the framework of traditional worship and procedure or you can do without external behaviors. Even if you refer to yourself as a Christian, a Jew, a Buddhist, a Hindu, a Moslem, or by whatever affiliation; realize this to be an external relationship. You can be loyal to your traditional practices while inwardly remembering that you are a spiritual being without labels or dependencies of any kind. When you depart this world upon death of the body you will not take your affiliation with you. When you experience transcendent states you have no awareness of relative limiting conditions. Pure consciousness is independent of relationships. While relating to the world we can of course play any role we deem useful and appropriate in order to function in society and assist planetary transformation.

The Seven Stages of Unfoldment and the Seven Vital Centers

Creatures and human beings have subtle, vital centers through which life forces or pranas flow to enliven and nourish their bodies. In the human body, these centers are more developed and organized, and along with the brain allow for expressions of progressively higher levels of consciousness. A commonly used word for these centers is *chakra*, which means "wheel." The spokes of the wheels are the frequencies of life force which operate through them.

Soul force enters the body at the medulla oblongata at the base of the brain, then flows to the higher brain centers and downward, into the body. The vital centers are astral

*The Seven Vital Centers in the Subtle Body
and Corresponding States of Consciousness*

CROWN CHAKRA Upper brain and beyond. Illumination, transcendence, absolute pure consciousness, soul liberation, spiritual freedom.

SPIRITUAL EYE Between eyebrows, reflection of the medullary center at the base of the brain. Access to inner planes, God-consciousness.

CERVICAL CHAKRA In spinal pathway, throat center. Cosmic consciousness, heightened powers of intelligence and awakened intuition.

DORSAL CHAKRA Between should blades, heart center. The "door" between higher and lower levels. Soul or Self-realization.

LUMBAR CHAKRA Middle back, fire center. Self-consciousness, sense of individual self, will and ability to use executive skills.

SACRAL CHAKRA Lower back. Subconscious states and their influences, sensory involvement, realm of fantasy, illusions.

BASE CHAKRA Bottom of spinal pathway. Unconscious states and their influences. Instinctive behaviors and attachments.

Note: Kundalini, the dormant potential soul force rests in the lower chakras and awakens with soul aspiration, devotion to God, prayer, and meditation, to vitalize the systems of the body and elevate consciousness.

or life force manifestations and through them forces flow to regulate internal processes. According to the soul's identification with the vital centers, so levels of awareness are determined and powers of perception and function are influenced.

1. *The Base Chakra*. At the bottom of the spinal pathway. Prana operating through this center regulates the body's gross (earth) matters. Prana frequencies here can sometimes be perceived as yellow light seen during meditation, as the sound of restless bees emanating from the chakra, and perhaps a sweet taste in the throat and mouth. Consciousness influenced by this center may manifest as anxiety about physical survival and welfare and desire to accumulate material things. Unconsciousness is the predominant state of consciousness. Even though one is awake and functional, intellectual capacities may be dull and intuition rare or unreliable. The religious impulse may impel one to identify with a belief system, a fundamentalist theology or philosophy, and perhaps with some hope of a comfortable, heaven-like afterlife as a reward for righteous behavior.

2. *Sacral Center*. In the spinal pathway at the lower back. Prana operating through this center regulates body fluids (water). Prana frequencies here can sometimes be perceived as white light (like a crescent moon) during meditation, as flute-like sounds emanating from the chakra, and perhaps an astringent taste in the throat and mouth. Consciousness influenced by this center may manifest as being attracted to sensory stimulation, enjoyment of relationships and things, and to be subject to misperception or illusions. Confusion can result. Subconscious tendencies are influential, powers of discrimination and determination may be flawed and fantasies may be falsely assumed to be intuitive perception or guidance.

The religious impulse may impel one to be fascinated with psychic phenomena, the unusual, the different, the fanciful. Some astral perceptions may be present but will tend to be mixed with base chakra influences and influenced by egoism. Many partially awakened persons at this level erroneously assume themselves to be sincere students on the enlightenment path when, in fact, they are caught in their own illusions.

3. *The Lumbar Chakra.* In the spinal pathway in the middle of the back, opposite the solar plexus. Prana operating through this center regulates biological transformations (fire). Prana frequencies here can sometimes be perceived as red light seen during meditation, harp-like sounds emanating from the chakra, and perhaps a bitter taste in the throat and mouth. Consciousness influenced by this center may manifest as self-determinism, desire to master the environment or create a personal reality, and functional abilities to self-responsibly fulfill purposes and be in control of circumstances. Egoism may still be dominant but a degree of comprehension of mental capacities and ability to exercise them may be present. Alert, awake, self-consciousness is the predominant state of consciousness. Subconscious and unconscious tendencies can still be influential. The religious impulse may impel one to study metaphysics and other systems of philosophy and thought, the understanding of which promises empowerment and control. One who is accomplished at this level may erroneously assume to be enlightened and in charge of personal affairs.

4. *The Heart Center.* In the spinal pathway between the shoulder blades. Prana operating through this center regulates the circulating properties in the body and gaseous substances (air). Prana frequencies here can sometimes be perceived as bluish light seen during meditation, the continuous (unstruck) sound of a gong emanating from

the chakra, and perhaps a sour taste in the throat and mouth. Being halfway between the three lower centers and the three higher ones, it is called the "door" between outer and inner realms. Egoism is less here, and the religious impulse may impel one to study higher metaphysics, dissolve ego boundaries, make a commitment to spiritual practice and growth, and be a surrendered disciple on the enlightenment path. Love of God may be pronounced and renunciation of all that seems to stand in the way of God-realization is contemplated. Prayer and meditation are attractive and enjoyable. Compassion awakens and one wants to serve others and the cause of evolution. One wants to do God's will.

5. *The Throat Center.* In the spinal pathway behind the throat. Prana operating through this center regulates the fine forces and properties in the body (space). Prana frequencies here can sometimes be perceived as misty-greyish light with bright sparkling lights, the sound of rolling thunder or the ocean's roar, and perhaps a pungent taste in the throat and mouth. Keen powers of intellect are usually manifested, enabling one to discern subtle workings of Nature and somewhat comprehend the reality of God and the categories of cosmic manifestation. Thinking is entirely rational; fantasies are absent. The religious impulse may result in one becoming a true philosopher-seer. Cosmic consciousness is spontaneous. The devotee sees the oneness of life.

6. *Spiritual Eye Center.* In the forehead, between the eyebrows. Pranas here are reflected from the medullary center at the base of the brain. This center is associated with the exercise of pure will and meditative contemplation. The light seen here may be a dark blue orb with a golden halo, the blue centered with brilliant white light. Gold is said to be the frequency of Aum or Om, the Word, the creative force pervading the universe. Blue is said to

be the frequency of God's universal intelligence, which regulates cosmic forces in manifestation. White is the frequency of the original, pure force-consciousness preceding manifestation. Established at this chakra, consciousness is removed from world identification. The soul is Self-realized and able to comprehend the reality of God and awaken to full God-realization.

7. *Crown Chakra*. Related to the higher brain and often illustrated in portraits of saints as a light around and over the head to indicate illumination of consciousness and transcendence. Established at this level of consciousness the soul is fully liberated.

You can experiment to experience immediate, even though perhaps subtle in the beginning, adjustments of mental attitude and states of consciousness which relate to the vital centers. When your feelings are centered in the two lower ones you may feel more body conscious and sense oriented. When you feel more established at the lumbar center and solar plexus you may feel more personally powerful. When your attention and feeling is at the heart center you may feel more devotional and compassionate. When you bring your attention and feeling up to the throat center in the neck you may feel more objective and discerning. When awareness is more focused at the spiritual eye center you may be more intuitive and removed from disordered thought processes and emotional changes, more Self-aware. With awareness in the crown center you may feel more spiritually free and expansive.

When we are more body oriented and involved with the senses and with relationships and endeavors, our vital forces are usually more focused and flowing through the lower centers even though we may be rational and purposeful and have some inner sense of our spiritual identity. In the absence of awakened spiritual consciousness, soul force is so obviously identified with the body that much of it is dormant. Dormant soul force is kundalini (Sanskrit), evolutionary force within us with potential. Its spontaneous awakening contributes to our psychological transformations as a result of its actions. This force is our own—it is not an outside power. It is the same force that pervades the universe and empowers it, as well as enlivens all of Nature. It is the power of God in us and the universe.

Kundalini is quickened within us when we aspire to spiritual growth, cultivate devotion to God, and nurture soul qualities. It can also be awakened in us when we associate with spiritually awake people. Their more fully expressive soul forces blend our dormant ones, stirring them into action. Visits to temples, shrines and ashrams where the energies are more refined, can also enliven our soul forces. Devotional prayer, superconscious meditation, and the practice of meditation techniques which can be learned from a proficient teacher, can give us more conscious control over our soul forces.

Purification of consciousness, transformation of mental states, and even regeneration of the body can be experienced as a result of cultivating higher states of consciousness and allowing kundalini to be more expressive. By attending to our spiritual practices and living a balanced, ordered life, our nervous system is nurtured, becoming more refined and capable of processing higher states of consciousness. This is one of the secrets of facilitating more rapid spiritual growth.

We may sincerely desire improved understanding of God and universal processes, we may honestly want to grow spiritually, but if our nervous system is overstressed and we are subject to mental confusion and conflicted emotional states, higher states of consciousness cannot be processed by the nervous system. Our earnest efforts to grow spiritually are then thwarted—not because God is not responsive to us, and not because we are undeserving of grace, but because we cannot experience higher states of consciousness or be responsive to grace because of our inner restrictions. All mystical and enlightenment traditions teach practices which can be helpful to devotees who want to help themselves to spiritual growth by self-responsibly removing restricting influences from their lives. These being removed, flows of creative forces complete the refinement of the nervous system and illumine the mental field so that enlightenment spontaneously occurs.

Everyone, if they live long enough, in healthy, supportive circumstances, will experience progressive spiritual growth because of the soul's innate inclination to awaken and become increasingly conscious—even if they are not consciously thinking about higher possibilities. However, the average person experiences episodes of psychological trauma, confused mental states, circumstantial challenges of one kind or another (including those which threaten survival, illness, addictive relationships and behaviors), and periodic episodes of physical death and often reincarnation. So spiritual growth is impeded in many instances. Enlightened seers, those who see from a higher perspective, teach that with concentrated endeavor it is possible to experience accelerated spiritual growth and realize God in one incarnation.

To be sure, perhaps not all who aspire to full illumination of consciousness in the present incarnation will be successful, but they will accomplish more than they would have accomplished had they not chosen the direct path and given themselves to it with one hundred percent devotion. What is your dream, your highest aspiration for spiritual growth in the time allotted you in this world? If it is full God-realization and liberation of consciousness, accept it as your major purpose and do everything you can to allow it to unfold. Listen to the words of the wise and model your life after their example, instead of listening to the baseless talk of persons who know little or nothing about higher possibilities and whose lives are determined by their moods, whims, and self-centered preoccupations.

I tell you truly, that one of the major obstacles to spiritual growth is the inclination to adapt to behaviors common to the conditioned human experience—to be average, to get by, to fit in, to be a reasonably content human being instead of awakening to one's full potential and actualizing unrestricted soul capacities and abilities. Most people who are not growing spiritually simple do not want to.

Once on the spiritual growth path, other obstacles may be encountered but cannot stand against right resolve, right application of known principles, and prudent exercise of common sense. One may be tempted to become overly preoccupied with psychic phenomena or mental abilities. Another may be attracted to the possibilities of telepathic communication with "advanced spiritual beings" in subtle realms. There can be no doubt about the fact that waves of blessings can be transmitted through planes and dimensions by saints and if we understand this process we can be open to it. But some sincere devotees, as well as persons given to fantasies, erroneously assume themselves to be in contact with such beings when they are really deluding themselves and accessing subconscious memories, as well as opening themselves to the possibility of having hallucinations. Such involvements should be avoided if satisfactory spiritual growth is to be allowed to unfold. The spiritual path is not one of escape from reality, but to a more comprehensive realization of it.

We need not deny our natural urges which impel us to live normal, functional lives. They only need to be refined and regulated so that we can choose how best to live. We naturally have an obligation to attend to matters which relate to our physical security and wellness, and to the security and well-being of others for whom we are responsible. We naturally desire to experience relationships and enjoy life. We naturally desire to satisfy our wholesome curiosities. We naturally want to achieve worthwhile goals and fulfill purposes. And we should do these things, while, at the same time, being intent upon becoming learned and cultivating our spiritual capacities. What is destructive is to allow senses to be unregulated, self-centeredness to determine choices, and preferences for circumstances which provide a modest degree of human happiness to take precedence over the really important matters before us.

It is not difficult to awaken to Self-realization and to enjoy a conscious relationship with God. We only think it is when fixated in egoism and attached to our illusions and misguided behaviors, and when we are feeling sorry for ourselves and give in to moods of hopelessness. Spiritual growth is not only natural and possible, it is destined—therefore, why not get on with it? All problems associated with conditioned states of consciousness will be easily solved as higher states of consciousness are allowed to prevail.

While attending to all necessary and chosen duties, feel yourself to be a participant in the creative processes while knowing that a Higher Power is working through and around you for your, and Its, highest good. Renounce the concept of duality, that God and Nature are separate entities and that God and you are separate beings. Learn to acknowledge oneness and to be in the flow of life. Plan for the future while being open to unplanned good fortune. Have an understanding of your role in the universe while being attentive to present conditions. In this way your everyday living experience becomes a conscious, spiritual exercise and your spiritual growth is fully supported and facilitated even while you participate in relationships and activities consistent with your present station in life.

Meditate daily to experience superconsciousness and to allow its healing, redeeming influences to flow into your mind, body, and affairs. When superconsciousness is coincidental with your normal waking states while you are active, you will experience cosmic conscious states at all times. From this level of awareness you will steadily awaken to God conscious states and all necessary knowledge will be revealed to you. You will have actualized salvation, the condition of being saved from suffering due to ignorance. Nothing in your past experience can influence you. Nothing in your present experience can bind you. Awake in God you will be liberated in Truth.

5

Meditation for Life Enhancement and Illumination of Consciousness

> May that soul of mine which mounts aloft
> in my waking and sleeping hours,
> an ethereal spark from the Light of Lights,
> be united by devout meditation with the
> Spirit supremely blessed.
>
> *The Rig Veda*
> *(the oldest known sacred text)*

> By deep meditation and living for God alone,
> calm the waves of thought and desire that condition
> your perception of reality. Then you will behold
> everything as it really is.
>
> *Paramahansa Yogananda*

If you are not already a dedicated meditator, include the following routine in your daily schedule for six weeks and notice the difference it makes in your life. You do not have to have a profound metaphysical understanding to benefit from this practice; nor is the procedure one which requires undue effort to acquire proficiency. The key to success in practice is doing it.

The process does not need to be discussed or analyzed,

for it is already being used by millions of people around the world who care enough about themselves, and about wellness and functional living, to make it a priority practice on a once or twice a day schedule.

If you already meditate as a spiritual exercise you should include this process as the preliminary stage leading to more profound contemplation. You, also, can benefit from the relaxation response and mental calm that will result. Then, stress-free and devoid of conflicted mental and emotional states, deeper meditation will flow more smoothly. Proceed like this:

- Retire to a quiet place where you will not be disturbed for at least 20 minutes (longer if you are an advanced meditator and your routine will require more time). Sit upright in a comfortable, relaxed posture. Close your eyes and let your awareness flow to the area above your eyes, in the forehead, and upper brain. Let any concerns about your personal condition, relationships or projects, drop away.

- Let your breathing flow naturally. After a few moments, when you feel somewhat centered, introduce a word or word-phrase of your choice into your awareness. When you inhale naturally, whenever it happens, mentally "listen" to the word or word-phrase. When you exhale, when it happens, mentally "listen" to the word or word-phrase. Your word can be of your own choosing: God, Peace, Joy, Om, or any word with which your mind is comfortable. If using a word-phrase it can be Om-God, Om-Christ (or any saint), Om-Peace, or any words you feel are right for you. If you have been initiated into mantra meditation by a qualified teacher, use your mantra.

- Continue with the process, allowing yourself to become relaxed, mentally calm, and emotionally settled. After a while, if the word or word-phrase drops away leaving you in a conscious, relaxed state, just sit in that silent condition until you feel inclined to conclude the practice session. Allow at least fifteen or twenty minutes to become relaxed and peacefully centered.

- *Optional Conclusion*: Conclude with a verbal or mental prayer of thankfulness to God and appreciation for life and living. Think of all the people of the world with love. If you have problems to solve or decisions to make, sit in the silence for a while longer and contemplate those matters, allowing yourself the opportunity to reasonably determine possible solutions or right actions. Be optimistic, happy, feel yourself to be in the flow of life, and intuitively sense that you are becoming increasingly attuned to universal rhythms.

Approximately 20 minutes, at least, is the recommended duration for relaxation and inner calm for life enhancement purposes. You will of course meditate much longer if you are intent upon exploring higher superconscious states and beyond.

Let yourself experience the process, then go about your usual scheduled or chosen routines. Avoid anxiety about results. Don't talk about your meditation perceptions or the results of practice with others. (You may, if desired and if possible, occasionally discuss your practice with an experienced meditator whose life reflects wellness and order, for the purpose of reassuring yourself that you are practicing correctly.) Suitable times to practice are early in the morning before starting the day's routine of activity, and again in the afternoon or evening, or once a day whenever you choose as the most suitable time.

The regular practice of this simple process will enliven your body and mind, order your thinking, help you to effectively manage stress, strengthen the body's immune system and slow biological aging processes, refine the brain and nervous system, and awaken regenerative forces that will contribute to overall wellness and balanced function of glands, organs, and systems of the body. Even nonreligious persons can practice this technique with enjoyment and benefit greatly as a result. Devotees of God will find its practice to be compatible with traditional or preferred modes of worship.

Understanding the Meditation Process

Meditation is nothing more than allowing our innate urge to have awareness restored to total wakefulness to be fulfilled. Because of long habit, when we relax and become internalized, we tend to identify with subconscious and unconscious states and go to sleep. When we meditate, we allow ourselves to relax and withdraw attention from external circumstances while remaining alert. Then, no longer disturbed by outer conditions, we are aware only of our moods and thoughts. When these become subtle and cease to be dominant, we can rest in a state of relaxed, alert awareness and experience preliminary superconscious states. From here we can proceed to more refined states of consciousness.

Because of being accustomed to relating to mental processes we may, when attempting to meditate, tend to continue with our preoccupation with them. However, to meditate successfully we must be willing to learn to disregard mental processes and the moods they generate. When streams of thoughts and their fluctuations cease, and we remain consciously alert, superconsciousness and mental illumination is possible. The light of the soul, our luminous consciousness, is often prevented from being expressed in the mental field because of emotional restlessness and the persistence of thinking activity. This is why we may find it difficult to successfully meditate.

We often mistakenly presume our feelings to be proof of our aliveness and our thoughts to be evidence of our existence or reality. Yet, a few moments of reflection will reveal to us that we stand somewhat apart as the witness of our moods and thoughts and are, therefore, not them. Without this Self-observation we may erroneously assert, "Without my feelings and thoughts I will not be me!" This is of course far from the truth. The *us* of us is ever the same as pure consciousness, having existed prior to identification with mind and body, existing now as a specialized unit of pure consciousness, and certain to exist forever with or without a relationship with mind, body, or relative expressions of Nature. It is this real, permanent beingness of us that we want to consciously experience and realize during meditation and after interludes of meditation.

It is helpful, when meditating, to remember that the forever Self of you is pure consciousness and that meditation is the process which enables you to consciously, unmistakably know this. Any meditation process we use is merely for the purpose of removing our attention from all that we are not, in order to experience what we are.

Meditation, then, is not to be confused with any method of mood alteration or mental conditioning. It is possible, by an exercise of imagination and will, to induce pleasant moods and create interesting mental states which may be mistaken for higher states of consciousness. While these may be satisfying alternative episodes removed from ordinary states of consciousness and everyday realities, they will be but illusory preoccupations which prevent the unfoldment of more desirable superconscious states. So long as we are involved with mood-making, visualization, or mental preoccupations of any kind, we are not experiencing life enhancing superconsciousness. We may, of course, use our imaginal capacities to begin the meditation process, but will eventually have to depart from such activities if higher states are to be allowed to unfold.

Some meditators experience spontaneous meditation from the outset, without having any difficulty in internalizing attention and withdrawing it from sensory awareness, moods, and thought activity. They just sit in the silence and let the process proceed. This is the easiest way to meditate. They then almost immediately become aware of themselves as beings of pure consciousness. As this awareness becomes established, they become settled in Self-realization, absolute knowledge and experience of themselves of consciousness only. From this state they can gently contemplate higher realities, the reality of God and the field of unbounded, pure Existence-Consciousness, and experience and realize these levels.

For devotees who meditate easily and spontaneously, all that will be necessary is to do it on a regular schedule while remaining alert to subtle adjustments in states of consciousness. Just sitting in the silence for extended durations of time, watchful and responsive to what occurs while being open to progressive unfoldments and the possibility of instantaneous illuminations, will be sufficient for them. Their holy desire to know freedom, gentle persistence in practice, and God's grace, will ensure steady spiritual growth and final liberation of consciousness.

For devotees whose meditation practice is not so easy, knowledge and practice of techniques can be helpful. It should be understood that meditation techniques are preliminary to the natural flowing of the meditation process which will follow once the practice of technique has served its purpose. Keep in mind from the outset of meditation practice, that any techniques or processes which may be used are for the purpose of inducing relaxation, inward turning, and ordering and clearing of the mental field so that meditation can proceed without disturbance. They are not for the purpose of creating artificial mental-emotional states which may be mistaken for spiritual experiences.

If love for God is the dominant urge to God-realization, prayer can be the most direct approach to contemplative meditation. For this, prayer for the purpose of God communion is the immediate accessing process. Simply pray from the heart until there is no longer any inclination to pray. Then, be still, absorbed in your love for God and surrendered to God's way with you. Sit in the after-silence and tranquility of prayer for as long as inclined. Do not give up too soon. Wait upon God until you experience a soul response, until you feel soul satisfied.

It is helpful to have become informed ahead of time about the reality of God, your real nature as a spiritual being, and the characteristics of higher states of consciousness: superconsciousness, cosmic consciousness, God consciousness, and transcendent states. You will then be more likely to know what is happening as you awaken through levels of consciousness, accurately determine your states of consciousness as they are experienced, and know what to do to allow higher states to unfold. Without this prior knowledge there may be a tendency to err in perception and become involved in illusional states of consciousness which can distort revealed knowledge and interfere with steady progress. To avail yourself of accurate information about these matters, read this book carefully, or valid sources of knowledge of your own choice. Do not go into the inner realms of consciousness with the simplistic assumption that even though you are ignorant of the facts of life everything will be revealed to you without your having had to prepare yourself by being armed with helpful information. All knowledge *can* be Self-revealed, but it is very useful to prepare yourself ahead of time by learning what to expect.

Without some knowledge of interior states of consciousness there is the possibility of erring in judgment. We may feel ourselves to be Self-realized when we are but experiencing and actualizing preliminary states of superconsciousness. We may think that minor ecstasies and perceptions of visions or inner light are proof of spiritual attainment. We may conclude that with a little knowledge we are now ready to go forth to share it with a waiting world. We may have delusions of grandeur, imagining that we have a special mission of which the world must immediately be made aware if it is to be saved. We may feel confident that we have attained the utmost degree of perfection and ignore our spiritual practices, and even disregard standards of behavior "which are for the unenlightened but no longer apply to us." In summation: we may be a little more aware but just as deluded as before. In the secular realm, a person would be thought of as emotionally immature and ignorant if he attempted to pass himself off as being accomplished in any field where prior education was a requirement for proficient performance, without first undergoing the education process. Yet this is often precisely what happens with many people who embark upon their Self-realization endeavors. They assume themselves to be so unique that they can proceed in their ignorance, and they usually fail to accomplish any worthwhile spiritual growth. The enlightenment path is subtle, so acquire as much accurate information as you can and be prepared to learn as you undergo progressive growth episodes.

The easiest meditation technique for most people to learn and practice is mantra (Sanskrit: *manas*, "mind, thinking aspect," *tra*, "to protect and take beyond") meditation. Since the changes and fluctuations which ordinarily occur in the field of consciousness are the primary obstacles to experiencing superconscious states, these must somehow be stilled or transcended. A meditation mantra is a simple word or word-phrase which is introduced into the mind to provide an attractive focus for our attention, so that awareness is removed from involvement with moods and thought activity.

Correct mantra meditation practice will not pacify the mind or further condition it. It merely provides the meditator the opportunity to intentionally disregard distracting moods and thoughts and to flow attention to clear levels of awareness. For beginning meditators and for persons interested only in the relaxation and life enhancement benefits of meditation, any pleasant word or word-phrase will do. For devotees intent upon higher superconscious realizations, Self-realization and God-realization, a mantra which inspires devotion and inclines attention to these higher levels of awareness is usually preferred.

A meditation mantra can be a meaningless word or it can be a word with a seed-meaning to be contemplated, comprehended, and realized. The words Om or God have seed-meanings and potency which can be discerned and experienced. Mantra is used until it is transcended; that is, until awareness flows spontaneously to higher levels of consciousness where the mantra is no longer needed as a focus of attention. By mentally listening to the mantra, the meditator's attention becomes so absorbed in it that no external (moods and thoughts are external to clear states of consciousness) condition is cognized. Unless one has been initiated into mantra meditation by a qualified person, any convenient word or word-phrase will do.

If initiated into mantra meditation, the prescribed mantra should be used because it is pregnant with potential. It is charged with the intention of the initiator and the energy frequencies which prevailed at the time of initiation. It may also have its own potency, as the words Om and other Sanskrit mantras do. Further, the fact of initiation means that the meditator has made a commitment to practice, a commitment to excellence in living, and dedication to spiritual growth and enlightenment. Therefore, the mantra of initiation will have special potency and special meaning which can enliven the meditator's mind and contribute to steadiness on the enlightenment path. Such mantras are considered as sacred vehicles of transforming power and should not be superficially discussed or shared with others who are not sincerely intent on a spiritual growth quest or who cannot use, or benefit from them.

Meditation, correctly practiced, results in unfoldment of superconscious states. Preliminary superconscious states may be attended by doubt: we may wonder whether or not they are legitimate even though we experience a degree of calmness and inner peace. We may experience degrees of superconsciousness even while subtle thoughts continue to flow and moods continue to fluctuate. Eventually, thoughts will cease and moods will no longer be compelling. This is the interlude during which to consciously rest in the tranquil stillness of meditation. At this time superconscious influences can pervade the mental field, brain and nervous system, and body. Their influences, being superior to normal waking states, subconscious states, and unconscious states, are enlivening and transformative. They contribute to orderly thought activity when thoughts are still present and after meditation, strengthen the body's immune system and slow biological aging processes, weaken and neutralize destructive mental tendencies, reduce cravings and desires which arise from restlessness, and contribute to balanced brain wave activity. The nervous system is refined, gradually making it more capable of processing higher states of consciousness during and after meditation.

If meditation is practiced correctly, on a regular schedule for several months and years, the influences of superconscious forces will naturally result in illumination of consciousness, orderly circumstances, and enlightened living. This will occur even for persons who are not yet purposefully on a God-realization quest, and will occur more rapidly for those who are.

Forget anything you may have heard, or may hear, about any discomforting effects of meditation. Correctly practiced, the results of meditation are entirely constructive. For a healthy-minded, God-inspired person, there is no possibility of becoming mentally and emotionally passive, neurotic, or involved with fantasies. With high resolve and right practice you will only become more conscious, more knowledgeable, healthier, and creatively functional as a result of your devoted meditation practice.

We must, of course, maintain a balance in our lives: a balance of activity and rest, of meditation and attention to duties and relationships, while being centered in Self-realization and purposefully involved with living a God-directed life. So do not think of meditation as an interlude of withdrawal from oppressive circumstances, a time of blessed relief from challenge which enables you to again confront and put up with the noise and nonsense of the world. It is such an interlude, but the idea is to be able to return to this-world involvement with peace of soul and knowledge of how better to relate to it. Immediate and long term results of superconscious meditation should be that our full powers of perception and function are introduced into everyday affairs so that in the here and now we experience enjoyable circumstances because of our expanded awareness and skillful performance of duties.

This side of the field of Existence-Consciousness we

live forever in space-time, in this or another realm. There-fore, be as conscious as possible and live in harmony with the orderliness of the universe right where you are. Ac-knowledge the certainty of future constructive un-foldments, to be sure, but do not make the mistake of being resigned to hopelessness while thinking of a distant future time or place when and where conditions will be better. You are an immortal, spiritual being with virtually unlim-ited capacities and abilities. Actualize your essential be-ingness, unfold your capacities, and express your abilities.

Meditation Perceptions and Progressive Revelations

The possibilities of meditation perceptions are varied. During early stages of practice you may experience inter-ludes of mental calm which will be welcomely satisfying. You may have visual perceptions of dreamlike phenomena because of accessing subconscious levels of mind. These may be somewhat revealing of inner conditions, as ordi-nary dreams can be, but should not be presumed to be divine revelations or astral insights. Accept them for what they are, mere mental phenomena which are not to be given undue attention. You may become aware of interior conversations, mental dialogue which persists because of mental restlessness. Ignore this activity. You may see panoramic vistas, beautiful scenery, endless sky, or more cosmic visual phenomena. Allow it to occur but do not focus on it. You will go beyond this stage. You may see brilliant light at the spiritual eye. If so, you can allow your attention to be attracted to it, just as you might listen to your mantra, for it can serve to keep your attention involved and removed from moods and mental processes. If brilliant light is steadily focused, gently allow your consciousness to merge with it while being willing to go into it and beyond it to whatever next unfolds. You may simultaneously hear, in the inner ears, subtle sound frequencies or a steady, flowing sound. As with the light, allow your awareness to blend with this sound while being gently inclined to know and experience what is behind it, to know and experience its origin.

It is important to remember not to become overly fascinated with visual or auditory phenomena, because no matter how lovely, interesting, or attractive it might be, it is not you, nor is it what you ultimately want to experience and realize. Any perception that you have which seems external to you as the observer, is fleeting. It is not the permanent reality you really desire to realize. Some meditators, lacking high resolve, allow themselves to dwell at these preliminary levels. They even find them enjoyable and return to them time and time again, instead renouncing them in favor of more expanded states of consciousness. They mistakenly assume themselves to be having real spiritual experiences instead of discerning the supportive causes of the phenomena.

Preliminary superconscious experiences often have supporting influences. This is acknowledged by enlightenment teachers. The Sanskrit word used to describe superconscious states is *samadhi*. When mental actions and fluctuations diminish and we experience degrees of Self-awareness and identification with higher states of consciousness we are said to be experiencing degrees of samadhi. Two categories of transcendental awareness are described: samadhi with support, and samadhi without support. When superconscious states have the support of moods, concepts, visual or auditory perceptions, or any aspect of Nature, they are described as being states of samadhi with support. When we experience our beingness as pure consciousness, or experience the reality of God directly, it is samadhi without supporting influences being present. So long as we are either observing ourselves in relationship to whatever is perceived, or so absorbed in the object of contemplation that we are no longer consciously experiencing or realizing what is occurring, it is samadhi with support. What is more desirable is to consciously observe superconscious perceptions and experiences while we relate to them, and then transcend awareness of anything external to us.

By becoming established in awareness of our being-ness, without reliance upon externals, we actualize Self-realization. This may be preliminary to perception and relationship with that which is greater that we are, God and the Absolute Field of Pure Consciousness. From this level, no longer dependent upon any aspect of Nature or mental perceptions, we can contemplate our relationship to God. At this level it may seem that God is external to us. We may know who and what we are as specialized units of pure consciousness but may yet not know the reality of God in its entirety. By contemplating the reality of God we can have episodes of attunement, experience, and insights leading to realizations of God. When God is realized we realize that God alone is the manifesting reality of Pure Consciousness and we are reflected lights of God con-sciousness. When our realization is complete, we are fully God-realized.

Many saints, seers, and sages, even though God-realized, are not fully so. They retain a degree of adoration of God, which keeps them somewhat separated from complete oneness, or they have not yet resolved to com-pletely surrender their sense of independence. Some, too, retain a degree of individuality in order to continue some contact with the manifest realms for the purpose of assist-ing the progress of evolution and redeeming souls. Or it may be that their role is nothing more than the will of God so that outer purposes might be fulfilled.

How to Practice Meditation for Illumination of Consciousness

Resolve to be enlightened in this incarnation. Resolve to meditate on a regular schedule. Follow through and be true to your commitment. With resolve and commitment, all other actions and experiences will follow and you will definitely realize your highest potential and actualize God-consciousness in this incarnation.

If you are a new meditator, review the processes until you know how to proceed. If you are already meditating on a regular schedule, review the processes to be sure you are on the right course and that you are practicing correctly. Even advanced meditators need to check their practice from time to time. At every stage of higher unfoldment it is well to examine what is occurring and know what to do to continue to the ultimate conclusion of spiritual practice.

If you are becoming more obviously large-minded, soul content, creative, optimistic, functional, trusting of life, compassionate and generous in relationships, you are actualizing your soul characteristics and capacities. If this is not happening, examine your outlook on life, your philosophical view, and your lifestyle (including behaviors and relationships) to find out why you are not growing in truth and grace. Then make necessary corrections by using your best judgment or engaging in further study.

Have no anxiety about the outcomes of your dedicated spiritual practices. And when you meditate, have no anxiety about immediate results or what might happen while you meditate. Just give yourself to the process. Your innate intelligence, the intelligence of God in you, will be your guide after preliminary stages have been surpassed.

You are on the upward way, so there is nothing to fear or to worry about.

Choose a meditation practice routine that best suits your purposes and your temperament. You will become proficient with practice and learn new procedures as you progress.

Select a specific time and place for your daily meditation practice. Then and there be resolved to be alone with God, with no possibilities of disturbance or distraction. You use most of your hours for activity and sleep: choose to set aside at least one hour a day for prayer, meditation, and divine contemplation. Since your life is not your own, but is God's life which you are expressing, neither is time your own and is to be used wisely. Even if you are a novice meditator, please know that the relatively brief duration of time you invest in meditation practice will result in such an abundance of positive benefits that you will soon realize what a good investment it is. Everything in your life will improve when you meditate, regularly and correctly, with an optimistic attitude.

Your meditation chamber can be consecrated as a sanctuary if you like. There, have a comfortable chair, or a mat or blanket if you prefer to sit crosslegged. You can also have a small altar, a table or something upon which to place pictures of saints or any items that may have religious or devotional significance for you. This will be a matter of personal preference, of course. Use that place only for prayer, meditation, and for any inner spiritual work you might do. If it is not possible to have a special place set aside for this purpose, if you prefer not to have one, any quiet place will do.

Proceed as recommended at the beginning of this chapter. After becoming relaxed and internalized, sit in the silence. Have an agreed upon duration for practice, whether thirty minutes or more. If possible, allow time to sit longer if you feel like doing so. If you are an experienced meditator, after sitting for a while in the silence and when thoughts and moods begin to intrude, again mentally pray or use your preferred meditation technique to become internalized, then continue to be surrendered in the silence. Maintain an attitude of alert watchfulness throughout, to ensure conscious participation.

The progressive stages to be experienced after you sit are: ordering of thoughts and relaxation, internalization of attention, concentrated flowing of attention to the object or ideal of your practice, absorption in that or steady meditation, the peak experience for that session. Sit for the duration of time decided upon or until it passes and you feel inclined to conclude your practice.

If you occasionally do not feel inspired when you sit to meditate, or if meditation does not seem to be flowing in a satisfying way, sit anyway. At least put in the time. It may be that during such occasions, when you least expect it, a useful awakening episode or breakthrough will spontaneously occur. On such occasions, even if thoughts and feelings are rebellious or an inspired mood is not present, at least be the master of your body and sit because you have agreed to do it. You will then cultivate the habit of fulfilling your intentions; moods and subconscious tendencies will be regulated; and your powers of self-determination will become more influential. Mastering restless urges, moods, and whims is important to spiritual growth as well as to success in all worthwhile endeavors, and an ideal opportunity to exercise self-mastery is during your daily interlude of meditation. It can be helpful to have a well-defined routine, one that works for you, and adhere to it with surrendered devotion to God.

Once a week, once a month, or on special occasions, schedule a longer meditation program for yourself. This will afford you the opportunity to go more deeply into God and to come to terms with your relationship with God and your world. Special occasions may include intervals during the year when you feel the need to have a private retreat, to ground yourself more firmly in the Infinite and rededicate yourself to God-centered, purposeful living. This can be whenever you feel it would be useful. Meaningful times may be during your holy day season, at the beginning of a new year, or before or on your birthday. Going more deeply into God during these significant times can be psychologically healing and transforming as well as spiritually useful.

You may want to occasionally meditate with friends or associates who share your spiritual interest. This useful practice can reinforce the endeavors of everyone in the group. However, avoid dependency upon others and be willing to meditate on your own on a regular schedule. For group meditation practice, just come together at an agreed upon time, sit in the silence for an hour or so, conclude the session and resume your normal routines. Avoid superficial discussion of meditation practice or philosophical views. Let your inner experience be personal and private and your outer life and behavior reflect wisdom and appropriateness.

Expect regular meditation practice to result in beneficial changes in your life and open your consciousness to higher realities and awareness of God. Do not expect to meditate on a regular schedule and be able to continue in a routine of personality-centered behaviors, relationships and activities, because this cannot possibly be so if you meditate surrendered in God. Your awakened soul capacities and the persistent influences of superconscious forces will definitely result in psychological transformation, elevate your consciousness, change your outlook on life, improve your powers of intellect and intuition, and reveal to you your major purposes. The more Self-realized and

God conscious you become, the more you will be impelled to live a conscious, intentional, egoless life. If this is not what you want, then avoid spiritual studies and practices. However, if this *is* what you want, and in your heart you do, make the most of your present opportunity by seeing to your complete spiritual education as soon as possible and including meditation practice in your daily routine. Know it for what it is: the most beneficial, entirely constructive, life enhancing, and soul illuminating activity you can choose to experience.

Note: The guidelines provided in this chapter will enable you to experience satisfying spiritual growth as you continue to meditate on a regular schedule. Your innate intelligence and God's grace will guide you. If you have the opportunity to be personally instructed in meditation practice, be sure the person you accept as your mentor is well qualified and demonstrates in his or her life evidence of a reasonable degree of God-realization. If you are a new meditator, you will benefit by reading my book *An Easy Guide to Meditation*. For more advanced study and practice I recommend *Life Surrendered in God*, my commentary on Patanjali's *Yoga Sutras*. Both titles are published by CSA PRESS, Lakemont, Georgia.

6

How to Pray: With Results Following

And all things whatsoever you shall
ask in prayer, believing, you shall receive.
The Gospel According to Saint Matthew 21:22

From all blindness of heart, from pride,
Vainglory, and hypocrisy: from envy, hatred
and malice, and all uncharitableness,
Good Lord, deliver us.
The Book of Common Prayer

"Prayer," wrote the nineteenth century poet James Montgomery, "is the soul's sincere desire, uttered or unexpressed; the motion of a hidden fire that trembles in the breast." Even if not performed as a formal act of petition, almost everyone prays for help in times of trouble or during more inspired occasions when communion with God or the object of prayer is earnestly sought. It is to our personal and spiritual advantage, then, to know how to pray effectively.

Our prayers are not always answered and communion with God is not often experienced because we are too habitually conformed with the attitudes and behaviors common to the secular world. We need, therefore, to learn to pray in a higher dimension, to elevate ourselves into the levels of primary causes which determine and influence effects in the objective realm and which can be our access to expanded states of consciousness. Effectual prayer is an action, a procedure, a process which removes our awareness from illusions and allows us to clearly see and experience that which is more desirable and ultimately liberating.

As we become familiar with the lives of saints we discover a common behavior pattern—that of frequent prayer and meditative contemplation. They may pray to experience deeper communion with God. They may pray for understanding. They may pray for divine intervention in the lives of persons who are in trouble. They may pray for world peace and harmony among nations and groups. But they do pray. If saints and spiritual masters pray, how much more do we need to pray and to commune with God!

If we have nothing in our world of everyday experience for which to pray, or if we are confused and have no specific prayer purposes, we can always pray for more vivid awareness of the reality and presence of God. In fact, this should be done before praying for anything else, because the more anchored in God we are, the more likely we are to know what to pray for, and why and how.

We may fail to experience desired results of prayer because of not praying with a surrendered heart and a pure mind. Or it may be that we are praying for the impossible—attempting to change other people who do not want to change or cannot change to suit our purposes because they are working out their own destiny in relationship to God and the universe, or praying for results which are contrary to the orderly workings of Nature. Or it may be that we are inexperienced with the prayer process and have not yet learned to go deep enough into God consciousness, to the Source from which "all things possible" grace flows.

Sincere, surrendered prayer is always beneficial, never harmful, and is often dramatically productive of results. Therefore, we can only benefit from daily prayer practice. Religious leaders must pray in order to remain open and responsive to God's leading. Business people should pray in order to be led to render true service and be successful. Regardless of your present circumstances or station in life, you need to learn to properly pray. Children and young adults should be taught to pray, in order to assure their emotional maturity and spiritual growth, and to learn how to make right choices and live productive lives.

Pray first for God communion. Then if there are specific needs, pray for them to be met, and they will be met in just the right ways. It may be that you sometimes need help in resisting temptation of one kind or another. Perhaps you are tempted to go along with peer group pressure, to abuse food or harmful substances, to think ill of others or to manipulate them for personal advantage. Or perhaps you are somewhat prideful because of your presumed knowledge and developed abilities and are inclined to exercise personal power for selfish purposes. If so, use your power of will to regulate these impulses and pray through the moments of challenge until you are again peacefully settled in soul awareness and in harmony with righteous attitudes and behaviors.

Realize that as your awareness of separate selfhood decreases, realization of the true Self of you and your relationship with God will increase. No one is sufficient unto themselves; God alone is our sufficiency and the sooner we acknowledge this the better off we will be. Since there is no power but that of God expressing, we should realize that when creative forces flow through us and results are not entirely constructive, it must be that there are yet some interfering mental and emotional characteristics within us which are filtering and adulterating the flow. We must then do what we can to further purify our minds and emotions to remove the restrictions which qualify Life's impulse to flawlessly express through us. We should pray that our minds and bodies be compliant, responsive organs through which higher purposes can be fulfilled.

We may feel led to pray on behalf of others whom we know to be in need, or who have asked for our prayer support. The most purely motivated and effective way to do this is to pray for their highest good rather than to exercise will power or imaginative abilities to create circumstances we think might be best for them. To do this, sincerely desire the highest and best for those for whom you pray, discarding from your mind and consciousness any belief or attitude of restriction or limitation. You are then, in actuality, clearing your own mind and consciousness of any consideration of lack, disease, or difficulty of any kind, and sharing your clear realization with those for whom you are praying. Even if you feel strongly about praying for specific results, when it seems that immediate intervention is necessary, add the thought-impulse, "If it is for the highest and best good for all concerned," or, "If it is God's will."

In referring to "God's will" in this instance, I am not suggesting a passive "whatever happens must be God's will" attitude, but a conviction that the Higher Power is working through and *as* the person for whom you pray, for their spiritual awakening and eventual illumination of consciousness. It is awakened spiritual consciousness that will forever solve another person's problems, just as it will your own. Willful or whim-guided, manipulative prayer is sorcery and cannot have long-term constructive results. It tends merely to keep us, and those who are influenced by our actions, involved in conditioned, self-conscious behaviors and relationships and does not contribute to spiritual growth or to truly satisfying outcomes.

When praying for outer results for yourself or for others, pray with conviction until you experience a vivid realization of release, soul joy and gratitude, then no longer be concerned about results. If results are not immediately forthcoming, do not despair. Having prayed in the right way, you have done your part. Leave the results to Providence.

There are several levels of prayer participation. How we pray may be determined by our degree of God relationship, our needs, or the inclination of the moment. We may pray only for a more complete experience and realization of God. This is the typical prayer approach prior to meditative contemplation and, indeed, many devotees pray only like this. Settled in the conviction that the deeper they go into God the more grace will abound and circumstances unfold in perfect accord without their having to define outcomes, they are content to be "lost in God" and accept whatever is provided in the way of experience and circumstances. For them, prayer interludes are occasions of sweet communion, after which they attend to duties and relationships with appropriate care while continually awake to the divine presence. Their increasing unfoldment of cosmic consciousness and God-realization is their dominant desire. Having sought, and to some degree realized, God, and living with soul-directed purpose, they have the full support of God and Nature and fulfill their destiny. Because they love God in the highest way, ego boundaries dissolve and while attending to necessary details they experience that Something Larger than they are is living through and as them.

When we feel somewhat separate from God and are aware of our needs, we may pray to have them met. It is then that we pray, believing, knowing that as we believe so shall we have that for which we pray. This is the prayer of faith, asking with perfect trust in God's limitless ability to meet us at our level of need in the most appropriate ways. This is the prayer process of asking and receiving and it works to the degree that we can believe and accept desired results. Continuing in this way we eventually awaken to the realization that all of our needs are provided in God's consciousness, which includes this and all universes, planes and dimensions—God being the omnidimensional Reality pervading the manifest realms—and eventually no longer need to pray for results because of our realization that everything is taken care of when we are God-realized. Until established in God-realization it is perfectly acceptable, even necessary and desirable, that we learn to pray, believing, with results following.

Many devotees who have a comprehensive intellectual understanding of God and frequent episodes of transcendent realization, but who also experience interludes of ordinary states of consciousness mixed with superconscious states, often enjoy occasions when they worship God. They know God to be a transcendent Reality as well as the Everything of the manifest realms, and that God is themselves, yet they take pleasure in devotional worship of God. They may observe rituals, sing or chant, pray to God as the transcendent Being or to one or several aspects of God. They do this joyfully because it provides them pleasure, keeps them in tune with the Infinite, purifies their mind and consciousness, and introduces divine qualities into their personal world. They may eventually live their lives as a total offering to God, which is the most perfect mode of worship.

The transcendent aspect of the Godhead is impersonal while realizable. It is possible to love the transcendent aspect of the Godhead while acknowledging the many aspects or modes of active expression of God as Nature at fine, subtle, and gross levels of manifestation. Until the

Absolute aspect of God is clearly apprehended, devotees
may feel it more satisfying to relate to God at a level which
is real to them at their present degree of awareness. They
may personalize God's aspects, thinking of God as Father
(First Cause, Ruling or Regulating Influence, Lord God),
as Divine Mother (God as Creative Force, the field of
Nature and its various cosmic forces and aspects), or in
any other imagined form which enables one to feel a vivid
sense of relationship with God. The imagined or conceptualized forms of God are our personally chosen aspects
which serve us as points of contact with Supreme Consciousness or the field of Existence-Consciousness.

   Christians often relate to God as a caring Father. Some
include prayers to saints or presumed saints. In many
cultures God is also related to as the Cosmic Mother—the
field of Nature being God in expression and all of it holy,
to be honored, respected, and nurtured. A Hindu might
relate to God in one or several aspects: as the remover of
obstacles; the provider of wealth, knowledge, or good
fortune of various kinds. An initiated disciple in a yoga, or
another tradition may relate to God through the guru or
spiritual teacher.

   It does not matter how we begin our relationship with
God, so long as our dedicated intent is to awaken through
the stages of spiritual growth to full God-realization. This
being the determining resolve, we are certain to apprehend ever more subtle aspects of Reality until we experience illumination of consciousness or enlightenment. It is
of course possible for one to remain at a level of dependency, even of superstitious belief, in relationship to personal forms or aspects of God, but this will not happen if
the devotee is resolved to "go all the way to God-realization" in the present incarnation. A surrendered devotee
will never allow sectarianism or prejudice to cloud his
consciousness and restrict spiritual growth.

The Many Ways of Prayer

Prayer at its best is interactive communion with God. The deeper we go into God consciousness, the more we are led by it to pray in the most useful ways. "Go humbly before the throne of grace," advise the saints. "Admit your nothingness and God's allness." There is no need for conflict about this approach, for our ego-sense is only a false sense of being and must be dissolved or renounced if God's reality is to be known and expressed in our lives. So long as we pray from an attitude of self-consciousness, we will be inclined to pray *to* God to receive something in return. It is more satisfying to pray *in* God, to be merged in God. But however you pray, do so sincerely with a surrendered mind and heart.

If you don't know what to pray for, but you feel the need to pray, just talk with God. Pray: "Lord (or however you relate to God), I don't know my own mind but I love You and want to know You. Awaken my soul, open my mind, cleanse my spiritual sight, reveal to me the way You would have me go. Show me what to do. Have Your way with me." Use your own words, your own thoughts, as your devotional ardor impels, as your awareness becomes elevated to ever higher levels of knowledge and experience of God. You will then know when to pray for results and when not to pray for anything but God's grace.

When praying for results, be sure you want them, ask for them, believe them to be yours, accept them in your mind and consciousness, and have no doubt in your heart about their outcomes. As you go deep in prayer you will arrive at that place of conviction where you know "It is done." You will be filled with gratitude, thankfulness, even joy. You will not have to ask again. You will serenely, patiently wait for unfoldments which must surely occur.

If you are unhappy, pray for peace of mind and soul

contentment. If you are fearful, pray for trust and confidence. If you are sick, pray for vibrant wellness and follow through with practical actions to help yourself. If you are lonely, pray for a more conscious, a more real, relationship with God and it will unfold. If you are experiencing limitations of any kind, pray for absolute freedom. If you need evident prosperity in your life, pray for it and accept the fact that the universe can and will meet your every need, on time, abundantly, and in the most appropriate ways. If you need employment, pray to be of service, to be fairly compensated, while you help yourself by making contacts and being open to all of the goodness life has available for you. When we pray for things, relationships, circumstances, personal conditions, for others, prayer results are always in accord with our adjustments in attitude and states of consciousness which enable us to see and accept desired outcomes. That for which we pray, if it is a real need or even a casual desire, is available to us. Prayer enables us to see this to be so and to claim it.

When we put our visualized needs, our prayer concepts, into Universal Mind they draw forth a response because our minds are specialized units of Universal Mind. The end results of prayer are always predictable but the means by which results unfold may not be known ahead of time. You may pray for harmony in relationships, for instance. You may change and become more adaptable, others may become more adaptable, or present relationships may dissolve and news ones formed. The results are satisfactory but the circumstances may not be what you thought they would be.

As our consciousness expands, we are able to see opportunities which before were not seen. As our consciousness is elevated to higher levels, we have access to knowledge and operational powers consistent with them. As we become more open to grace, events unfold to meet us at our level of need and people with whom we are to share fate and destiny come in contact with us.

As these things happen, be sure to retain your common sense, your powers of reasoned determination, to discern what is to be accepted and what is not. Do not blindly assume that every new circumstance in your life is meant to be, or that every new person you meet is destined to be your permanent friend or business partner. Use your intelligence every step of the way and accept into your life only that which is highest and best. Provincial, dependent, or grasping people tend to settle for anything that comes along that is new or different; discerning souls agree only to circumstances which enhance their lives and further spiritual growth.

As you become proficient in praying with results following, your every good desire or worthwhile intention will bear fruit without your having to resort to specific asking-prayer. Even so, still pray for a more complete relationship with God, for communion with God. By doing this, you will be assured of knowing the depths of the Ocean of the Spirit of God and will avoid wasting your life in superficial pursuits, grasping at things and experiences as though they were more important than higher knowledge and Self-realization. All circumstances of the phenomenal realms are ephemeral, fleeting, and insubstantial. We need to relate to the world but not be attached to it. Live easily and enjoyably in the world but be attached only to God. That is the way of true happiness and real fulfillment.

Until you are functioning at the level of spontaneous fulfillment of desires (and you will know when your are), be as specific and intentional as you need to be to satisfy your needs and accomplish your purposes. You may find it helpful to keep a private journal, in which you write your inspired thoughts, plans, and goals and projects. You may want to list your needs, keep a record of your prayer-for-results practice, and a record of when and how your prayers bore fruit. This can enable you to become more familiar with the prayer process and how it works.

You may find it helpful to write and verbalize intentional affirmations as a way of ordering your thoughts, regulating your emotional states, and opening your mind and consciousness to possibilities. To do this, in a quiet, private place, write an affirmation which best describes a realized outcome. Write in the present tense, not "I will be" but "I am." After writing the affirmation, speak it aloud with conviction. Then speak it softly. Then whisper the affirmation. Then let it float in your mind. Finally, let it become a realized fact. For instance:

"I am made in the image and likeness of God. All of the qualities and capacities of God indwell me. Everything in my consciousness, mind, and environment is now in divine order. Thank you, God, for this understanding. Thank you, God, around and within me."

For mental creativity:

"My mind is a portion of Universal Mind, the Mind of God. I use my mental capacities wisely, in harmony with Divine will."

For emotional stability and maturity:

"I am calm, confident, serene, and self-responsible. Grounded in the Infinite, I easily and appropriately process thoughts and feelings and relate to others and the world with compassionate care."

For physical health and vitality:

"My body is the temple of the Holy Spirit. I allow God to be glorified through my body temple. God's life is my life. God's vital forces circulate through my body to ensure total wellness, perfect function, and radiant vitality."

For harmonious relationships:

"Settled in Self-realization I respect all people and behold their innate divinity. I love others and others love me. I serve others and help them to their highest good. I allow God to help me to my highest good through people God chooses in my life."

For success in ventures:

"I am always in my right place in the universe and in harmony with God's will for me. I acknowledge the creative forces of nature as benevolent and fully supportive of my worthy endeavors. In all that I do, I am God-led, God-supported, and God-provided."

For prosperity:

"Life's innate inclination is to thrive, flourish, and to successfully fulfill purposes. I thrive, I flourish, I am successful in every way. I prosper abundantly because I flow with God's purposes for me."

Be willing to learn, to grow, to adapt, and to exercise your talents and abilities to help yourself and to nurture others and the world. Attitudes of dependency (except upon God) should be renounced or grown out of as you progress. Life is for living, so live it well, right here and

right now. As your consciousness expands and circumstances and events unfold about you, be sure to adhere to
your daily prayer and meditation routine. This will keep
you grounded in the Source and help you avoid becoming
too caught up in relationships and activities which may
become a distraction. Even while enjoyably participating
in life's drama, remember your ultimate goal of liberation
of consciousness.

Open Yourself to Life: As You are Blessed, be a Blessing to Others

As you become increasingly aware that you are provided for from God's infinite Being and Presence, be more
open to life, and as you are blessed, be a blessing to others.
Whatever you desire for yourself in the way of fulfillment
and good fortune, wish for everyone else for they are as
deserving as you. The universe, having the fullness of God
within it, can meet all legitimate needs and no person
needs to be denied.

Every day, when you conclude your interlude of meditative contemplation and attend to your personal, inner
work on your own behalf, be sure to include prayer for all
people, everywhere. The same realization of God you
experience for yourself, know on behalf of others. Let your
consciousness of the reality of God radiate out into collective human consciousness and planetary consciousness.

When possible and when so led, assist others in practical ways to have their needs met. To the extent possible,
encourage people you know to acquire a spiritual education, to be informed of the reality of God and how to grow
in grace and Truth. God has already given you everything
and now you know it. Help others to know it too.

7

The Spiritual Basis of Real and Permanent Prosperity

The softest things in the world overcome
   the hardest things of the world.
Non-being penetrates that in which there
   is no space.
Through this I know the advantage of
   taking no action.
   The Way of Lao-tzu (7th century)

Take heed and beware of covetousness:
for a man's life consists not in the abundance
of the things which he possesses.
The Gospel According to Saint Matthew 12:15

Outer demonstrations of the prospering effects of inner, awakened spiritual consciousness can be: predictable success in personal endeavors, enhanced well-being, immediate availability of all necessary things and circumstances, thriving conditions, ease in ability to function, good fortune, optimum health, spontaneous fulfillment of desires, and boundless creativity.

Contrasting conditions, when awakened spiritual consciousness is lacking, or is partial but clouded by prevailing mental misconceptions or emotional conflict, can be: failure in spite of best efforts, want, lack, inner and outer confusion and limitations of various kinds, dysfunctional behavior, misfortune, uncertain health, difficulty in having desires fulfilled, and only occasional and often misdirected surges of creativity. Healthy-minded people naturally prefer prosperity to its opposite circumstances.

If healthy-minded people naturally prefer to prosper, why are not all who desire prosperity actually demonstrating it? The problem cannot be because of any deficiency in the universe or that the prosperity process operates only for some of us but not for others. If this were true, the process would be flawed and our honest endeavors to demonstrate prosperity would be subject to chance. We could never be certain of the outcome of our best efforts. The plain, simple truth about prosperity is that the prospering laws, or principles, of the universe are impersonal, infallible, and accessible to anyone who learns how to cooperate with them. What is helpful to remember is that there is no lack in the universe because the universe is a full manifestation of That which produced it out of Itself. To demonstrate real and permanent prosperity it is only necessary for us to clearly understand how the prosperity process works and be willing to let it express in our lives. Many decent, sincere people are not prospering because their understanding of themselves as spiritual beings is flawed and they are not yet clearly aware of their real relationship with God and the world. They are in need of further spiritual education, and if they are reasonably healthy-minded they will do all within their power to acquire it. On the other hand, there are many people who partially understand that they are spiritual beings in relationship with God and natural laws, but psychological unrest, subconscious conditionings, and egocentricity or self-consciousness may be preventing them from having easy access to levels of awareness they aspire to realize.

We can only demonstrate or actualize (experience in fact) that which we can accept in our experience. No matter how sincerely we may yearn for peace of mind, emotional calm, physical health, supportive relationships, effortless unfoldments of circumstances and fulfillment of desires, if we cannot feel comfortable with these conditions and circumstances—if we cannot accept them as being natural and appropriate for us—we will tend to deny them expression. Such denial may take the form of conscious or unconscious avoidance of the constructive experiences we say we desire or intentional or unintentional indulgence in self-defeating behaviors.

It is not that God, or anyone or anything external to ourselves, prevents us from demonstrating prosperity. God as-life-expressing is the prosperity process and if we are not open and responsive to the flow, it is only that we have yet to learn how to come into relationship with it. If we are not demonstrating prosperity it is because we do not yet have a prosperity attitude and a prosperity consciousness. Our mental attitudes determine how we view ourselves in relationship with the world (and God) and our states of consciousness determine what can be included in our field of awareness. Rather than debate the matter of whether or not a universal prosperity process exists, we are better advised to improve our understanding and put it to the test of experience to find out for ourselves what is true. Any resistance we might have to doing this is but a reminder that even though we may claim that we desire improved circumstances in our lives, we are not always willing to improve ourselves! The natural law of causation underlying the prosperity process is that outer fluctuations and adjustments of circumstances always conform to our mental states, states of consciousness, and behaviors. What we *are* determines what we do and experience.

We are ever relating to one thing, to consciousness in

unmanifest states and to consciousness manifesting as various forms and circumstances. The material substance which forms our bodies and the things we relate to every day—food, clothing, houses, tools, money, the air we breathe—is actually consciousness-as-energy expressing in space-time. God's manifesting energy is the substance of everything in the universe, formed and unformed. (This means that right where we are, the allness of life is present. Acknowledge this fact, and never again think or say that you don't have anything or that your needs cannot be met. You do have everything, now, and so does everyone else.) We are already provided with all of the resources we need. If we don't think we are, if we don't know we are, the problem is our misperception of what is so—and misperception of what should be obvious is illusion. Awaken from the illusions which cloud awareness and all problems are forever solved.

We are spiritual beings in a spiritual universe. Since the worlds are produced and maintained by God, this must be so. If we have forgotten our essential reality it is only because of having become identified with matter, conflicted mental processes, unstable emotional states, unregulated sensory impulses, and outer circumstances. I emphasize the spiritual basis of real and permanent prosperity because without spiritual awareness our fleeting demonstrations of prosperity, whether spontaneous unfoldments or of our own intention, will not have a foundation in understanding and cannot be permanent. They will be subject to changes which correspond to our fluctuations of states of consciousness, mental states, and behavioral modes.

When we are spiritually resolved we desire more than comfortable interludes of human happiness. We want to be Self-realized—we want full realization of God and whatever that realization might spontaneously unfold in our experience. And if we are intent upon demonstrating real and permanent prosperity, we will not be satisfied until conditioned states of consciousness are transcended, Self-realization is stable, and God-realization continuously prevails.

With progressive spiritual growth we discover that we are effortlessly impelled to think and behave in ways which are in harmonious accord with Nature's laws and forces and circumstances which provide us opportunity for fulfillment in all aspects of our lives. We become increasingly knowledgeable about how the prosperity process operates. We learn by experience that we are attuned to universal rhythms, and that since the universe is maintained and nourished by an Enlivening Life-Power, so are we. We comprehend that because we are more God-conscious and in the flow of evolution's transformative currents. All that is necessary for our well-being and fulfillment is freely provided.

The spiritually useful approach to living is to accept the ideal of total wellness and functional freedom as being most desirable. Many who affirm their desire for illumination of consciousness are actually behaving as though life were a burden, as though waiting for death to release them to an imagined heaven, or to wherever their idea of improved circumstances might be. They are not preparing for their future by living consciously and responsibly in the present. They are not taking advantage of their existing opportunity to learn the prosperity process, to grow spiritually, and actualize their soul capacities. They are often content to cope with circumstances, to survive, while making excuses for their immature behaviors and finding fault with their circumstances. Their spoken words reveal their illusional mental states. They say: "I have a lot of overcoming to accomplish. I was not taught to live successfully when I was young, so I don't know any better than to behave as I do. I am a product of my past experiences. I never had any positive role models. I would do better if I were not addicted to my habits. There are many things I'd like to do but I don't have the time—or money, or friends, or knowledge." They behave like this because they are self-centered, fixated in egoism, and are using their superficial involvements with "spiritual" studies and practices as an escape from having to confront life as it is and come to terms with it.

We should be able to function as freely in this world as in any other we might know about or can imagine. Subjective laws of Nature are superior to objective circumstances, and when we really understand them we should be able to function with ease. In fact, we often do this without always clearly comprehending the prosperity process. For instance: we have all experienced occasions when our desires were easily fulfilled, when a mere gentle wish was sufficient to bring them into manifestation. Or an experience, circumstance or relationship was desired and without any conscious effort on our part it was made possible because circumstances "just happened" to unfold in supportive ways. This occurs because every impulse of desire is the seed of potential fulfillment of desire. Desires are self-fulfilling and are inclined to produce their specific effects unless they are suppressed because we deny them expression, neutralized because we renounce or discard them, or modified because of new choices we make.

The metaphysical law of causation is that subjective causes produce objective effects: states of consciousness and mental states precede physical conditions and circumstances. Subjective causes are primary; objective effects are secondary. Therefore, when we want to demonstrate spiritual growth, peace of mind, emotional contentment, radiant physical health, supportive relationships, success in planned ventures, and ideal circumstances of every kind, we have but to purely desire these results—remaining firm in the knowledge that the impulse innate to our desires is the self-fulfilling action which will blossom as orderly circumstances and conditions.

What about the time factor in relationship to fulfillment of desires? This will depend upon the level upon which actualization is to occur and the circumstances relating to it. For adjustments in states of consciousness and mental states, results can be immediate. Physical healings and adjustments in personal circumstances and relationships can also be immediate—so quickly demonstrated that they might be thought of as miracles. Or results may be slower if resistance to change is influential. For instance, we may desire to experience superconscious states when meditating but have difficulty doing so because of emotional unrest or mental restlessness. However, by facilitating deep relaxation, calming the mind by regulating breathing rhythms, or by prayer or contemplative meditation, obstacles to spontaneous superconscious perceptions can be removed.

Adjustments in mental states can usually be facilitated easily by letting go of unwanted attitudes and states and assuming ones which are deemed more desirable. Even an experience of unplanned good fortune can result in a sudden shift to more expansive, constructive mental states and elevated states of consciousness.

The way to proceed is to learn how to adjust states of consciousness and mental states at will, then let experiences and circumstances be determined by them. With practice, it is possible to always maintain spiritual awareness and constructive mental states without need for immediate external supportive circumstances. To do this is to exercise faith, for faith is literally the substance of what is to unfold in space-time. Desires which require the support of physical circumstances for their manifestation will express when ideal conditions prevail: time must be allowed for physical strength to be recovered, study and practice must accompany learning, and certain projects will require more planning and perhaps the cooperation of others. However, the unfoldment of outer circumstances is only the creation process necessary for pure desire to be manifested in obvious form.

Real and permanent prosperity is realized when we are where we are supposed to be in life's unfolding drama, doing what we are best qualified to do and with all needs easily and appropriately satisfied. Prosperity is not defined by an excess of things we might appear to possess. If resources are needed to fulfill purposes, we should have them, with minimum effort necessary to acquire or maintain them. Real prosperity is not always a matter of having what we want when we want it—for if we are not emotionally mature our wants may be virtually insatiable—but of unfailingly having what we need when we need it.

The universe provides for us because it is a continuum: one unified, functioning system which is self-contained and forever in process of transformation. The varied aspects of the universe are but categories of manifesting forces of which the whole of the universe is comprised. Our physical bodies are made of the elements of Nature and the cosmic forces which pulsate in space flow through us. Our minds are individualized units of a universal mind-stuff from which we receive impulses and into which our thoughts blend.

Since the universe is what it is and does what it does, we are linked with its processes at gross, subtle, and fine levels. We need to cooperate with Nature, not selfishly use it. We need to learn how to dance to universal rhythms instead of struggling against the tide of evolution. We need to learn how to creatively interact with universal mind and be responsive to its spontaneous support of our legitimate needs and pure desires.

The source of everything in manifestation is God and it is in the source we need to be understandably grounded. Circumstances will change, human relationships will be formed and discarded, economic trends will continue to fluctuate, climate patterns will vary, but the underlying consciousness of the universe will remain the same—just as in the midst of change and transformation we, at the soul level, remain the same.

What others who are not grounded in spiritual awareness experience, need not be your experience. Changes in your life can be seen for what they are: adjustments of events and circumstances in your permanent demonstration of good fortune. A job layoff, a business slowdown, an unexpected severance of a relationship—these and more will later be seen as growth opportunities, as blessings in disguise, when you are grounded in spiritual awareness and have faith in the prosperity process. As you proceed, knowing and believing, you will discover that a Higher Intelligence knows more than you do about how to live your life and how to make all necessary arrangements for the fulfillment of life's purposes through you.

What about the practical things that need to be done? Learn what they are, how to do them, and expedite them with excellence. Learn from successful people, then innovate and adapt to suit your personal needs and creative urges. Along with proficiency in practical matters, acquire a metaphysical understanding of the operations of success principles. Experiment with the laws of causation as you understand them, while being open to discovering more efficient ways to function. You will learn that effort is not necessary in the prosperity process: that understanding, cooperation, and faith is the better way.

Since the universe is already providing us with all necessary resources, we have only to learn to accept what is available by recognizing it. To the degree that we do this, outlets for flows of Nature's support of us are provided. What useful, creative ideas do you have? Express them. What needs do you have? Make them known to the universe by acknowledging them and expecting them to be met. What necessary or worthwhile service can you render to others and to the cause of evolution? Render it with love and without attachment to the results of your thoughts, prayers, or actions.

You are not a body or a mind: you are consciousness expressing through body and mind. Therefore, whenever necessary, remind yourself of the truth about yourself and adjust your states of consciousness and mental states accordingly. Use your creative imagination to expand awareness to levels from which you can easily see all possibilities. If change of any kind is needed in your life, assume viewpoints and mental attitudes which correspond to the changes you need and outcomes you desire. To actualize what you want to experience you must be expansive enough in consciousness and mind to easily accept it in fact. This being accomplished, desired circumstances and experiences then flow into expression. When understood and applied, the creative process operates flawlessly.

Imagination is a creative faculty of the soul. Whatever states of consciousness or levels of awareness you can imagine and assume, you can realize. I am not here referring to created mental states which, if produced and identified with, would result in fantasy or hallucination, but to conscious adjustment of states of consciousness by using imagination as a technique or procedure.

Train yourself to intuitively apprehend full spiritual awareness and accept as natural your ability to exercise intelligence. Assume yourself to be in command of your thoughts, moods, and behaviors and let them reflect your intentions. See through circumstances if they are not what you feel are best for you. You will then know how to do whatever is necessary to help yourself. You will experience unfolding events that conform to your clear perception of possibilities. It is not that you will always be causing effects—though this will sometimes happen— rather, you will more and more live in the consciousness of fulfillment and all necessary adjustments of circumstances will harmoniously occur as a result.

You can train yourself to see your relationship with the world as you would like to experience it, during the course of daily activities. Just remain inwardly calm and soul-centered as you proceed. You will experience the "dream" character of your world and learn how to relate to it with higher understanding.

Be sure to meditate every day until you experience deep mental calm and soul peace. Sit for a few minutes in the tranquil after-effects calm of meditation. During this interlude, know that your inner awareness is illumining your mind and beneficially influencing your body. Extend your awareness to include your environment and feel yourself to be in harmony with the rhythms of Nature. Feel yourself to be in your right place in life's plan. Accept emotional maturity, physical wellness, supportive relationships, and success in all endeavors. Conclude with a few moments of radiating knowledge and awareness of love and good will to all people everywhere. Be happy. Be thankful for the gift of life and for God's goodness. Maintain your awareness of your relationship with God and the universe as you resume normal activities. If all personal circumstances are orderly, be thankful. If they are not, they will definitely change to conform to your inner knowing, belief, conviction, and realization.

There are many practical procedures recommended to encourage people to be more open to their available good. Some of them are effective to the degree that one has faith in the process. For example: some religious scriptures recommend, "Give generously, to others in need and to worthwhile causes, and as you give, so shall you receive." *As you give* is the key, not what, how much, or to whom or for what purpose. It is assumed that giving will be thoughtful and appropriate. When we give generously according to our means, with an attitude and feeling of gratitude for being able to give, our consciousness expands and we experience a more obvious attunement with the prosperity process. The moment we give is the moment of blessing because our actions are evidence of our consciousness of having, because we are in harmony with life. With right understanding we do not give to receive; we give out of our realization of the fullness of the universe.

I have heard "prosperity teachers" say, "Give and it shall be returned to you tenfold!" Why only tenfold? Why not one hundredfold, or a thousandfold, or more? Giving to receive is bargaining with the universe and if that is the level of one's understanding it can be a beginning in the direction of unfolding a prosperity consciousness—but it is still a dualistic approach. It is based on the attitude of "I am separate from the universe and must perform a ritual to invite its participation." We are already one with the universe, and its fullness is immediately available to us in relationship to our acknowledgement of it.

Another religious practice in relationship to giving and receiving is tithing. A *tithe* is a tenth part of a whole or ten percent. Some Bible students quote The Old Testament (*Malachi 3:10*): "Bring ye the whole tithe into the storehouse, that there may be meat (food) in mine house, and prove me now herewith, saith the Lord of hosts, if I will not open you the windows of heaven, and pour out a blessing, that there shall not be room enough to receive it." Beautiful, even stirring words, but which should be understood in their context to the circumstances and culture during which they were written.

Under Levitical law the tithe was a form of taxation required of the Hebrews, usually a portion of their harvest and of their herds of cattle and other animals. It wasn't a freewill offering, token donation, or charitable contribution. Because theirs was a religious form of government, many assumed their giving to be a gift to God. Their tithe-tax was really a way of supporting their government and thus making provision for the community, much as we are asked to pay taxes today.

Many religious people do affirm that generous giving, whether an actual ten percent or more or less, provides them an opportunity to engage in disciplined giving. As a result, they feel better about themselves, they are able to do some good, and their more intentional use of available resources enables them to be more consciously responsible in using their money, time, and energy wisely. They learn to invest, to save, to avoid waste, and in many ways be more in charge of their affairs. If we believe that cheerful giving will result in an increase of money, good fortune, and other things and circumstances we consider to be evidence of a prosperity consciousness, the process will work according to our expectation and degree of acceptance. If we are not open to the prosperity process, giving will be merely a duty, helpful to those benefited by our giving but not always resulting in obvious prosperity circumstances for ourselves. The best way to give is to do so prudently, as a matter of choice, while being thankful for having the means and the freedom to do so.

Life is good to us; why shouldn't we be good to life? Life blesses us through others. Why shouldn't we let life bless others through us? It is from God through the universe that all provision flows. We own nothing. We only have the use of resources. We are stewards, not owners. In a higher sense, as spiritual beings, all that is manifesting is ours to wisely use. Problems occur when we allow egocentricity to rule our consciousness, causing us to become grasping, clinging, and attached to things and circumstances.

Responsible use of resources, without attachment to them and without attachment to the results of our creative actions, is the ideal. All manifest forms come out of an inexhaustible field of Pure Consciousness. Cosmic forces flow from this field and express variously, but the field is never depleted. Just as we came from inner space and will one day return to it, so everything in manifestation came from inner space and will flow back to it. The heavens and the Earth will pass away but Consciousness remains forever.

To actualize prosperity in your life, provide an outlet for its expression. Instead of struggling to demonstrate mastery of physical, mental, or metaphysical laws of causation, prepare avenues through which the prosperity process can flow and unfold by cultivating your creative abilities. Learn how to make useful contributions to society and the world. Discover your major purposes and fulfill them. You will then be in harmony with evolutionary forces. You will experience that when evolution is allowed to follow its inclinations, it will bring together the people and the resources to accomplish its purposes. You, being a part of the unfolding process, will then naturally experience prosperity in every way. Along with ordinary unfoldments, you will realize accelerated spiritual growth because psychological restrictions will be removed and your transformational forces will be fully expressive.

8

The Usefulness of Healthy, Long Life with Enlightened Purpose

This (is the) noble eightfold path...right views,
right aspirations, right speech, right conduct, right
livelihood, right endeavor, right mindfulness,
and right contemplation.
Buddhism, Pali Canon

Be ever involved with God. When not meditating,
be active for Him. And when meditating, offer your
mind to Him in the same spirit of service, with
alert attention. Be ever involved with God, and with
doing good for others.
Paramahansa Yogananda

As spiritual beings, we are immortal. We have always lived and we will live forever. Our bodies, except for their cosmic forces, are not immortal, nor are they meant to be. We are not forever residents of Nature's realm, the field of experimental life and the playground of souls. But with right attitude, right understanding, and right endeavor, we can function freely in this world for as long as we have enlightened purpose—until purposes have been fulfilled and our highest potential for spiritual growth has been realized. This is the real value and ultimate usefulness of healthy, long life in the material universe.

The World Health Organization has defined *health* to be not only the absence of disease or infirmity, but as a state of optimum physical, mental, and social well-being. This is the ideal for the average person. For the exceptional person who is desirous of demonstrating total fulfillment we add awakened spiritual consciousness, because total health must include soul enlightenment.

One hundred twenty-five years is the generally assumed potential life span for human beings. Few instances of longer durations of human life have actually been verified. There are stories, of course, some of which I believe, about certain mortal-immortals who maintain their physical forms for hundreds, even thousands, of years but even they will eventually discard them. There are also some people who presently hope to live forever in the physical body or transmute it into finer essences and take it with them to subtle planes; a vain hope that only reveals their lack of understanding of the processes of spiritual evolution. Most human beings, unaware of their spiritual potential or caring little about it, live ordinary sense-oriented lives and sooner or later die to the world because of accidents, disease, diminished capacities, tiredness, or boredom.

At least 70 percent of the causes of illness and premature physical death are preventable: the majority of diseases and disabling circumstances being directly related to life style behaviors and unwise food choices. When we do not know how to live in a manner which supports wellness, or do not care to do so, we tend to adapt to behaviors commonly accepted as normal. We do not then cultivate habits which would enable us to live in accord with Nature's supportive influences. We allow ourselves to dramatize neurotic and psychotic behaviors. We do not manage stress, but allow it to accumulate and disrupt psychological and physiological function. We do not eat correctly. We do not exercise and rest on a regular schedule. We do not cultivate our mental, moral, and spiritual capacities. And we do not live with firm resolve and high purpose. We do almost everything wrong, yet our innate drive to live and prevail somehow keeps us going. And, more often than not, we live to an average age of 75 or 80 years—not always in a healthy, happy condition, of course, but sometimes so.

I am not here emphasizing marginally healthy, long, relatively unconscious, egocentric life, but radiantly healthy, long life with enlightened purpose. And what are some of the constructively useful outcomes possible for us when we live like this? What could we accomplish if we took leave from the attitudes, beliefs, and behaviors which are known to be repressive and restrictive to the soul's innate urge to express freely and transcend all boundaries of presumed limitations? How far could we then see with our soul vision? How high could we rise in consciousness? How influential could we be in contributing to the uplift of others and to the ongoing, transformative actions of evolution? Yes, what could we do, and what could God do through us, if we simply turned away from all unrighteousness and chose to live righteously?

Healthy, long life with enlightened purpose provides us the opportunity to have a knowing, harmonious relationship with the universe and the full support of Nature. It enables us to come to terms with life, to realize that we do have the resources and means to satisfy our legitimate desires and fulfill personal and destined purposes. It results in peace of mind, enjoyable relationships and experiences, progressive spiritual growth, and God-realization in one incarnation. Now do you understand the usefulness of it? Do you feel a real soul response, a happy willingness to live like this?

A large percentage of the world's population grow up ignorant of the facts of life. They remain self-centered, grasp at fleeting promises of pleasure or happiness, are sense-bound, psychologically conflicted, and generally dysfunctional. They erroneously assume themselves to be mere biological entities, at the mercy of forces and circumstances over which they have little or no control, and resigned to inevitable, progressive deterioration of their faculties because of old age, then death. For some, extended life span is desired because of their will to live in spite of life's imperfections. Others, fearing death and possible after death states, cling tenaciously to physical life. Many, weary of coping or of the routine, welcome physical death as an opportunity for unconscious rest.

But physical death is not the end of us. We came from inner space and to inner space we will surely return when our purposes for being here have been fulfilled. Having existed prior to birth of the body, we will continue to exist when we depart it. In the meantime, we have lessons to learn, growing to experience, and duties to perform.

As souls, reflected lights of God's consciousness, we are inclined to identify with the manifest realms in accord with our states of consciousness and urges or desires. We can only function at levels of consciousness which are experienced as real by us and relate to the environment as we perceive it. We are, therefore, in this world because this is where we feel most capable of functioning or because of our desire to be here.

I have heard people say, "I would rather not be in this world. I would rather be somewhere else." To which, I ask, "Why do you not want to be here?" And, "Where would you rather be?" While we may be able to suggest any number of reasons for not wanting to be in this world, I have never heard anyone clearly define and describe a more suitable, alternative place. True, unless we are illumined we are all "homesick for heaven," for our awareness to be restored to the intuitively apprehended or dimly remembered condition of enlightened fulfillment. What is not always grasped by the intellect is the fact that it is possible to realize spiritual fulfillment while embodied; that enlightenment is not determined by our location in space-time, but upon our degree of awakened spiritual consciousness.

If all we had to do was to get through this incarnation with reasonable success, then die to the world and awaken to ever higher states of consciousness, there would be little need to aspire to spiritual growth. There are undoubtedly some souls who are in the world because of their casual interest in it, or because they are completing some agreed upon duties—and they may know this—but most are here because they need to learn how to grow spiritually.

Most souls experience successive rounds of physical birth and death because of their confused states of consciousness and attachments to relationships, sensation, and illusions. The exacting, causative laws of correspondences (as within us, so without) determine our circumstances. The only way to reliably adjust circumstances is to adjust our mental states and states of consciousness.

We suffer the consequences of delusion, not because God wills it, but because unconsciousness results in misperceptions, errors in judgment, and faulty behaviors. We experience the constructive results of more enlightened perceptions and behaviors because of being able to more intelligently relate to the world. Ours is not a happy state of affairs when we are unaware of the facts of life, when we do not know how to help ourselves or improve our circumstances. Thankfully, if we are even partially conscious and desirous of further awakening and improved function, there is a way out of the darkness of unknowing, into the light of clear understanding. It is the way taught by seers and sages: acceptance of the fact of our need to awaken and grow; commitment to learning and growing; and practical application of procedures and processes which allow episodes of transformational experience.

Healthy, long life provides us time to engage in self-analysis, neutralize our traumas and conflicts to facilitate psychological wellness, fulfill the desires we feel to be useful to satisfy, keep our agreements with others and meet obligations and responsibilities, further our spiritual growth, and make constructive contributions to society and the planet. These being accomplished, we no longer have any compulsive ties with the mundane realms and can remain here only for the purpose of selfless service while completing the soul enlightenment process.

We then live with higher understanding, cosmic conscious and God-realized, no longer compelled by karmic conditions (unconscious and subconscious drives, tendencies, desires, and conflicts) but flowing in harmony with the rhythms of Nature, responsive to the directive impulses of Higher Consciousness and maintained by God's grace. Having had prior knowledge and experiences of subjective states of consciousness and higher orders of reality because of expanded states of awareness and meditative contemplation, eventual departure from the body will be experienced as but a shift of viewpoint. Perceptions and experiences which follow will be in accord with capacity, interest, and need. We will be able to realize God conscious states as our capacity to do so allows. We will tend to be attracted to subtle realm circumstances which interest us. Or, we will be attracted to the highest levels of God-realization and transcendental states.

Guidelines to Healthy,
Long, Purposeful Life

Be as clear as possible about your major purposes in
life as you proceed with routines and practices to facilitate
total wellness and longevity. You will then be more inspi-
rationally motivated and conscious of why you are implementing life enhancement processes. Disease-free, functional living without a clear sense of realizable purpose,
while of some value in that it may afford opportunities for
normal evolutionary growth, will not provide awareness
of meaning to your life that is important to have. Use the
planning forms provided at the end of this chapter to chart
your course in life while, at the same time, being open to
the unplanned good fortune you will certainly experience
because of Nature's supportive influences and God's grace.

Two vital factors for healthy, long life, over both of
which we have control, are *mental attitude* and *life enhancing activities.* Optimism, the basis of hope and faith,
should be habitually cultivated until it is the dominant
mental attitude. Cheerfulness and optimism actually
beneficially influence the body's chemistry, enlivening its
functions and strengthening the immune system. Pessi-
mism, fear, doubt, depression, mental and emotional
conflicts, and other negative states depress the body's
immune system and disturb normal biological functions of
organs and glands. Life enhancing activities keep us in the
flow of relationships and cosmic forces which contribute to
our total wellness and encourage biological systems to
function harmoniously.

Why is it that some people are old at what should be
healthy, functional middle age while others are youthful
into their seventh, eighth, and even ninth decades or
longer? Genetic predisposition may play a role, but not as
much as we may too quickly presume. *The determining*

factors are more likely related to mental attitude, states of consciousness, the kind and amount of suitable physical activity, and diet. This is the opinion of many physicians, and the testimony of an increasing number of men and women who are enjoying healthy life into what use to be considered advanced years. For many people, who have traditional ideas about aging, the various symptoms believed to be associated with it begin to manifest because they expect them to! Aging then becomes a wish-fulfilling prophecy: what is anticipated is demonstrated in fact.

In an article published in a national magazine, a medical doctor wrote of his extensive studies on aging. He found that if you list all the changes in muscles, bones, brain, cholesterol, blood pressure, sleep habits, sexual performance, psychological characteristics, and other symptoms— and compile a list of similar changes which result from physical inactivity, there is a striking comparison. Indications are that many of the bodily changes we tend to contribute to normal aging processes are in fact caused by disuse, by inactivity. The five components of what may be called the Disuse Syndrome are cardiovascular vulnerability, musculoskeletal fragility, obesity, depression, and premature aging—all of which we can do something about.

Physical conditioning determines how well our bodies transport oxygen necessary to good metabolism. Exercise improves the body's ability to take in and transport oxygen to the blood stream. By exercising regularly, and maintaining muscle mass, metabolism is more efficient. Exercise also keeps our bones in better condition, stronger and with minimal loss of calcium. Without exercise our energy reserves diminish, we "feel older" and more tired, and tend to become more easily depressed.

Your personal exercise routine can be chosen to suit your needs and capabilities. Usually, the best approach is to stimulate the systems of the body but not overchallenge them. It is not advisable to exercise to the point of exhaustion. Several times a week, with an occasional day of rest, exercise to the point of light perspiration around the head and neck and enforced deep breathing, staying within your own known limits. The purpose of exercise is to enliven the body's systems, not to overly tire or injure them.

Brisk walking, for one or several miles per session, is one of the better exercise routines because it provides the body with oxygen, cleanses the systems and blood because of improved circulation and deeper breathing, strengthens the muscles involved, and improves cardiovascular function. After several minutes of brisk walking (or other chosen exercise) the brain secrets a chemical substance which causes a natural elevation of moods and more optimistic mental states.

Another psychological benefit of exercise, especially walking, is that it removes us from routines and circumstances, from stress-inducing conditions or interludes of boredom, and brings us into more direct communication with our bodies and our world as-it-is. We feel better and the world looks better to us when we go for an intentional, enjoyable walk.

When possible, exercise outdoors in fresh air, without wearing glasses of any kind. Thirty minutes to an hour of direct exposure to natural light is beneficial to the body. Full spectrum light, not necessarily in direct sunlight, is absorbed through our eyes and used by the pineal gland in the brain to regulate subtle biochemical processes in the body. Depriving the body of the entire range of the light spectrum can interfere with normal functions, weaken the immune system and contribute to various disease conditions. It is also a good idea to ensure full spectrum lighting in living and work environments and to use a variety of colors in your room decorating scheme. Consider full spectrum light as nourishing "food" for the body.

The upper body should also be adequately exercised on a regular schedule, to maintain muscle tone and mass. For this, stretching movements can be done, light weights can be used to provide mild resistance, or any suitable program utilized. More complete exercise routines may include bicycling, tennis, swimming, or whatever else is enjoyed. A daily or several times a week hatha yoga routine can be extremely beneficial for stretching and strengthening muscles, improving blood and lymph circulation, culturing the nervous system, awakening and circulating life forces or prana, inducing deep relaxation, and enlivening the body's regenerative energies. For persons unable to practice hatha yoga for one reason or another, a daily tai chi routine would be helpful for similar results.

It is estimated that one half of the functional losses that manifest between ages 30 to 70 are attributable to lack of exercise. When aging is accompanied by inactivity, it can result in the following declines: 1) Muscle fiber is lost at the rate of 3-5 percent a decade after age 30, leading to a loss of 30 percent of muscle power by age 60; 2) By middle age, blood vessels may narrow by approximately 30 percent. Between ages 25 and 60, blood circulation of arms and legs slows down by as much as 60 percent; 3) The speed at which messages move from the brain to the nerve endings decreases by 10-15 percent by age 70. Regular exercise has been shown to inhibit such declines in function.

Accumulated stress is one of the most disruptive and debilitating causes of psychological unrest and physical impairment. It disturbs mental processes, unsettles emotions, weakens the immune system, interferes with nerve impulses, upsets biological rhythms, and contributes to malfunctions of organs and glands. It can impair eyesight and hearing, reduce overall awareness and normal powers of perception, and increase the likelihood of our making mistakes and having accidents.

Stress accumulates in the body when we feel ourselves to be overworked, overtired, when circumstances seem to us to be overwhelming, and when we are unable (or unwilling) to process and comfortably relate to information which streams into our consciousness through the senses. Worry, anxiety, fear, despair, and a sense of hopelessness, can also cause stress to accumulate.

The first step to successful stress management is to learn to be Self-aware, to see ourselves in a right relationship with God and the universe, and to cultivate a dispassionate view of circumstances—to view ourselves and our environmental conditions with impartial calm. The immediate next step is to implement a total life style program which is entirely supportive of ourselves, which will enable us to experience orderliness, harmonious relationships, and appreciation for life.

Environmental circumstances which may overly challenge the mind and nervous system should be regulated. Too much noise, confusion, irrelevant conversation, disorganized activity, chemical pollution, exposure to magnetic fields (produced by electric power lines, computers, television sets, electric and battery powered household appliances, mobile telephones which emit microwaves) can disturb the body's delicate balance, injure the nervous system, and interfere with normal biological processes.

Regular physical exercise, a balanced, nutritional diet, enjoyable interludes of recreation, regular sleep habits, and orderly, purposeful living help us to successfully manage stress. Loving, supportive relationships also reduce stress, help to make life more meaningful, and contribute to psychological and physical health.

Daily meditation is the most convenient and helpful

stress management regimen. Mental calm and deep relaxation which results from correct meditation practice drains stress from the body, cultures the nervous system, enlivens mental creativity, and enables us to see ourselves in a better relationship with the world. We can then learn to be at peace within, regardless of external circumstances. Even if one is not presently intent upon an enlightenment quest, meditation should be daily practiced to nurture psychological health and improved physical function. Regardless of your chosen actions, remember that the Spirit of God is the doer of all things and that you are but a facilitator. You have a role to play but outcomes are not always in direct proportion to your personal actions. By playing your role in life with common sense, with right understanding, you will be able to relieve yourself of the burdens of worry and anxiety about the results of your endeavors. Therefore, while being self-responsible for your personal actions, let God handle the details.

Biofeedback training can also be helpful in educating us in the management of stress. It can provide actual experience of direct relationships between mental attitudes, states of consciousness, physiological states, and brain wave patterns. Once sufficiently trained, an individual may then monitor mental states, moods, states of consciousness, and physical states, adjusting them at will to allow optimum function. By becoming familiar with how attitude influences body chemistry and organic function, it is possible to acquire a considerable degree of conscious control over involuntary systems of the body and biochemical processes, and awaken and direct regenerative healing forces. The fine cosmic forces which regulate subtle physical processes can be consciously influenced by our thought impulses, imaginal states, and states of consciousness.

Other practical aids to managing stress and facilitating mental, emotional, and physiological orderliness are regular chiropractic adjustments, dry or oil body massage, firm but gentle self-administered foot massage, acupressure treatments, and other convenient alternative procedures which are known to be helpful.

It is important to remember that our self-care routines and practices are meant to assist us to healthy, functional living and are not ends in themselves. In fact, preoccupation with any regimen can lead to increased self-centeredness and avoidance of the real purposes before us. Know your self-care routines for what they are: practical aids to more expansive, enlightened, purposeful living and progressive spiritual growth.

Cosmic forces pulsing through the universe also circulate through our mind and body. When we are in harmony with cosmic forces around and through us, and the specialized cosmic forces within us are in a state of functional balance, radiant health is spontaneously actualized. Our minds are then calm, thoughts are orderly, physical systems function harmoniously, awareness is unrestricted, stress is minimal, perceptions are acute, and awakened spiritual consciousness is stable. Therefore, our life style choices and behaviors, and personal self-help routines, should be seen as adaptive modes which keep us open to the flows of cosmic forces around and within us.

Self-conscious, spiritually unawake people often erroneously think of addictions, disabilities, difficulties, and troubles as being natural to the human condition. They are normal to conditioned and deluded states of consciousness but they are not in accord with Nature's inclinations—which are to encourage function and growth. No otherwise useful self-care routine will be ultimately successful without a degree of spiritual awareness being realized by the person adopting it. Some constructive results may be experienced, of course, but for total success spiritual awareness must be the primary factor.

It is now known that many disabling conditions and diseases, including some of which are major causes of dysfunction and premature death (especially in the West and increasingly in many developing, industrialized regions of the world) are directly related to careless dietary habits. Among these are: coronary disease, heart attacks, strokes, diabetes, high blood pressure, and some types of cancer. Most of these conditions can be avoided by using common sense and adopting self-care regimens, avoidance of environmental pollutants, the cultivation of optimism and purposeful living, and by choosing a balanced, nutritional diet.

The foods we eat blend with our thoughts, desires, and states of consciousness to become our bodies. Ingested foods are transformed into plasma, blood, muscle, fat, bone, bone marrow, reproductive essences, and a final essence which enlivens the immune system and imparts to the body the glow of health. With increased spiritual awareness, this fine essence is supplemented by substances produced by the brain and glands which have regenerative influences. Transcendental forces actually become transmuted into fine energies which pervade and enliven mind and body.

A balanced selection of fresh, natural, pure vegetarian foods is the ideal diet for human beings. Our tooth structure, digestive organs, and psychological and physiological response to such a diet provide adequate evidence of its appropriateness. Animal products, especially their flesh, are not our natural foods and are best avoided. A motivating factor in choosing a vegetarian diet can also be our knowledge that, as a result of our choices, we are no longer even remotely involved in the mistreatment of other life forms. One of our guiding ideals should be that of avoiding harmful acts when at all possible.

Food preparation and consumption need not be complicated. Merely choose a variety of grains, vegetables, legumes, some fruits and nuts, and fresh, pure water, and utilize according to need. Since we do not all have the same psychophysiological constitutions, our food needs will vary. Attentive experimentation will reveal the most ideal and satisfying food plan for your own purposes. Of course avoid fads and fanaticism. It can, however, be helpful to learn about the chemistry of food preparation, and how best to combine food groups and bring them to the table with nutrients intact and available for assimilation.

Eat only when calm and quiet, and only the amount necessary. Excessive food consumption, even of nutritious meals, works a hardship on the body, tiring the systems and often resulting in an accumulation of undigested residues which impair normal function. Systematic undereating is recommended: ingesting a sufficient, varied quantity without overdoing it. This regimen has been found to extend the life span of some animals far beyond their normal range.

Complex carbohydrates, provided by whole grains, and taken with legumes, provide a balance of amino acids to assure protein requirements. Many newly decided vegetarians become overly concerned about obtaining adequate protein from a vegetarian diet. Under ordinary circumstances this is no problem. Most people, especially those who include meat in their diet, consume too much protein, the excess of which may be stored in the body as uric acid which causes the heart to be overworked and generally tires and weakens the body.

Grains can include: brown rice, millet, buckwheat, barley, oats, corn, and others of choice. Fresh vegetables can include: carrots, potatoes, cauliflower, broccoli, dark green vegetables of all kinds, cabbage, squash, and more.

Legumes can include: lentils, split peas, pinto beans, black beans, kidney beans, chick peas, and more. Flours can include: whole wheat, soy, rye, and cornmeal. For unrefined oils: safflower, corn, and sesame. Sweeteners, when desired in small quantities, can be: raw honey, maple syrup, or any natural product. Foods which prove disagreeable to your constitutional nature can be avoided.

Foods to avoid include: foods that are not fresh, including canned foods and foods which have been prepared and then allowed to become stale or undergo even preliminary phases of decomposition; foods and drinks containing concentrated sweeteners and that are excessively salty; foods and drinks with chemical preservatives, flavor enhancers, and artificial coloring; white flour products; white sugar; foods or drinks containing caffeine or other stimulants.

When preparing food, use the leaves and peelings of vegetables and fruits when possible, to obtain full nutritional value. Steam vegetables instead of boiling them, to preserve nutrients. Use iron or stainless steel cooking pots instead of aluminum or copper. Grains, legumes, and some vegetables, such as potatoes, require cooking to break down the cell structures so that nutrients can be assimilated, but it is usually best to avoid overcooking. When gathering, preparing, and consuming foods, give thanks to God for the generous bounty of the universe. Through food you are in direct rapport with universal forces. Honor yourself, honor the universe, honor the divinity of every person, honor all forms of life.

*How to Know Your Right Place
in Life and Fulfill Purposes
and Soul Destiny*

If you are already committed to a life of real purpose, continue with routines and practices which support your commitment. If you are newly resolved to live with real purpose, make all necessary adjustments to immediately conform to your choices. In this way, everything you do will be entirely supportive of all aspects of your life. If you are young in calendar years, your commitment to purpose now will enable you to avoid future problems and difficulties, and to avoid that saddest of all outcomes—a wasted life. If you are older, life style changes can be made just as easily; all that is needed are your choices and commitment to them. If you are elderly and know for certain that you are not long for this world, make peace with it and devote your time and attention to further spiritual growth so that your transition will be easy and comfortable as you move to a higher plane of experience.

Procrastination is a most obvious symptom of our denial of life. When we allow it to determine our behavior we refuse ourselves the very good fortune we really desire to experience. The happiness and spiritual freedom we innately desire is available to us now, for the acceptance of it. Expand your awareness beyond the conceptualized boundaries of one physical life cycle and realize that you are not really confined to considerations of relative time. Accept the reality of your being; that the true Self of you is spiritual, and all concepts, misguided desires, and habitual behaviors common to ordinary, conditioned states of consciousness will fall away. In one sentence I will give you the key to absolute spiritual freedom: *To be a Self-actualized being, all you have to do is know, feel, think, and act like one.*

Until we are stable in Self-realization, even with the best of intentions it is often easy to get off course—to become involved with moods, attitudes, relationships, behaviors, and activities which are contrary to our higher purposes. Unless we are grounded in the Infinite and ever responsive to inner guidance and in the flow of spontaneous unfoldments of events and circumstances, we need to adhere to routines of study and practice that can provide the support that can help us remain spiritually alert and focused on our purposes. For this, a daily self-care regimen, removed from outer influences, is the most beneficial. For this, adapt any of the following suggested routines in ways which best suit your personal needs:

1. *Early Morning.* The most ideal time because you will then be putting important things first in your life. You will be cooperating with Nature's daily cycle of awakening to activity, as well as preparing yourself for your own planned and unplanned activities. Awake from refreshing sleep, attend to bathroom needs and refresh yourself. While still quiet and calm, pray and meditate deeply for at least 30 minutes, or longer if you want to. Read scripture or inspirational/philosophical literature for a few minutes. If you like, practice a hatha yoga routine, then dress and start your day's routine of work or activity. If you prefer to practice hatha yoga or engage in other exercise routines later in the day, do so. Do what works best for you, with your spiritual practices and meditation as the foundation of your life.

2. *Afternoons or Evenings.* If you are not a "morning person," if your mind-body rhythms are not conducive to alert practice of meditation early in the day, at least pray for a few minutes when you first awaken, and schedule meditation in the afternoon or early evening when practice is more enjoyable and productive.

3. *Weekends and Holidays.* Use these occasions when you are relatively free from the demands of work and social obligations. Schedule an hour or more for metaphysical studies and deeper meditation. Over a long holiday weekend or at any chosen time during the year, schedule several days or a week or more for a private meditation retreat.

Absolutely resolve to attend to your wellness and spiritual growth practices. If you are not as healthy and spiritually aware as you are capable of being, you will not be able to efficiently fulfill your personal purposes or your soul destiny. If you want to actualize your soul capacities in this incarnation, adhere to essential behaviors and eliminate all nonessentials from your life. Decide how much time and energy to give to your intentional spiritual practices, how much time and energy to give to work to earn money or render social service, how much time to give to personal and family relationships, and how much time to further your secular and spiritual education. One hundred percent dedication on your part, and God's grace, will ensure altogether constructive results.

The way of enlightened purpose is not for weak-willed, small-minded, self-serving people. It is for those who are intentional, universal in outlook, and compassionately caring in thoughts and actions. If you don't want to grow spiritually, if you prefer to live an ordinary, illusional, self-focused life, admit it and accept the consequences. Just don't whine, complain, and blame God for anything you may experience or confront as a result of having made that choice. The far better way is to think about your relationship with God all of the time, to live your life in relationship to God all of the time.

Always be self-reminded that you are in this world to experience a harmonious relationship with the universe, satisfy your necessary desires, have adequate resources and means easily available to enjoyably accomplish your purposes, and fully awaken to God-realization. By doing these things you serve the cause of creation and fulfill your soul destiny.

Remaining steady on your true life path, you will experience progressive and accelerated spiritual growth. Dormant soul capacities will awaken and you will know how to allow them to express. Intellectual powers will improve and intuition will unfold. Knowledge of higher orders of reality will be revealed to you. Circumstances and events will spontaneously arrange themselves in harmonious, supportive ways. The enlivening influences of higher consciousness will inspire a flow of creative ideas and all of your thoughts, emotional states, and actions will be entirely constructive. Harmlessness, truthfulness, honesty, right use and transformation of vital forces will be natural to you, and you will be free from addictions and blind attachments.

You will be pure in mind, motive, and deed. You will be soul content, self-disciplined as a matter of choice, grounded in contemplative meditation, surrendered to God, and will compliantly live with absolute reliance upon grace. Regardless of prevailing societal or planetary conditions, you will live with higher understanding and your personal circumstances will always be orderly. You will be reconciled with the past, at peace in the moment, and assured of continuing good fortune. Exceptional powers, perceptions, and abilities will be natural to you. All of these unfoldments and characteristics are natural to the spiritually awake soul. Why not now?

Practical Application

Use the following planning forms to choose and implement life style changes and practical programs that will support your highest purposes and contribute to your spiritual growth. Do this when you are rested and quiet, preferably after an interlude of meditative contemplation when your mind is calm and your actions deliberate.

In a notebook or private journal, clearly write your responses to the questions and recommendations. Refer to your notes from time to time, to update your entries and to maintain your resolve. Feel yourself to be in relationship with the Infinite as you do this. Let your mind and consciousness be open to all the good that is now available to you. The universe is nourished by a Benevolent Power—cooperate with It.

Your self-transformation experiences, constructive changes of personal circumstances, and spiritual growth episodes will provide obvious evidence of the usefulness of living with enlightened purpose. Continue to demonstrate your awakened spiritual consciousness. The process will be an ongoing learning opportunity.

My Mission Statement for Fulfilling
All of Life's Purposes in this Incarnation
"I can see clearly now and I rejoice in understanding."

For our lives to be meaningful, they must have purpose. A mission statement is an intentional declaration of enlightened purposes. You need not know just how they are to be fulfilled in order to write your mission statement. Think about the years yet remaining in this incarnation and what you want to experience and accomplish. Write from your heart, clearly and concisely.

_____

_____

_____

_____

What can (will) you do to fulfill your purposes and allow life's inclination to completion of purposes be expressive?

_____

_____

_____

_____

_____

_____

My Personalized Spiritual Training Program
"I live, pray, and meditate in God."

The basis of total wellness and fulfillment of life's purposes is our commitment to study and practices which can facilitate our spiritual growth. Write your study and practice program and implement it immediately. If you are already a committed devotee of God, review your study and practice program and make improvements where necessary.

1. My choices of philosophical studies are:

_____

_____

2. My daily routine for prayer and meditation:

_____

_____

_____

_____

3. What, if anything, needs to be changed or improved?

_____

_____

_____

_____

My Psychological Transformation Program
"My mind is cleansed and spiritually renewed."

While purposeful living and spiritual practice can greatly contribute to psychological health, we can help ourselves by becoming aware of attitudes and emotional states that need to be examined and adjusted. While doing this, remember that you are a spiritual being with freedom of choice.

1. Attitudes and emotional states that need to be changed and what you will do to make necessary changes:

_____

_____

_____

2. Behaviors that need to be changed and what you will do to adopt more useful, constructive behaviors:

_____

_____

_____

_____

_____

_____

My Healthy, Long Life Program
"The radiant Spirit of God shines through me."

Everything we do should be supportive of our enlightened purposes and of spiritual growth. Natural, wholesome living confirms our high resolves and allows them to more easily be demonstrated.

1. If you are in need of healing, what will you do to be healed?

   _____

   _____

2. Write your exercise routine:_____

   _____

3. Write your nutritious food program: _____

   _____

4. Include anything else you are doing (or will do) to assist yourself to radiant wellness and to maintain it.

   _____

   _____

   _____

   _____

   _____

My Personal Prosperity Program
"God is the Source and Substance of my prosperity."

To *prosper* is to thrive, flourish and be successful in every way. When we are open to life, we experience the full support of Nature, enjoy cooperative relationships and experience rapid spiritual growth. Be willing to prosper. Accept the good that life is providing you now.

1. Clearly define any limiting attitudes or concepts which may be restricting the flow of prospering actions in your life. What will you do to eliminate them?

2. Clearly define any self-defeating behaviors or relationships which may be restricting the flow of prospering actions in your life. What will you do to change them?

3. What else are you doing (and will do) to open your mind and your life to prosperity? (Include your work or service rendered, savings and investment plan, charitable giving, and all actions which keep you in the flow of life's unfolding good.)

My Personal Excellence Program
"I use my abilities wisely and without restriction."

Skillful actions attune us to universal forces and their constructive, creative processes. We should become fully aware of our spiritual, mental, and physical abilities and express them freely.

1. What creative abilities are you now using for constructive purposes and how can you more effectively demonstrate them?

   _____

   _____

2. What latent abilities do you have which need to be more fully developed, and what will you do to unfold them?

   _____

   _____

3. What new skills are you interested in acquiring, and what will you do to acquire and proficiently use them?

   _____

   _____

   _____

   _____

   _____

My Hopes and Dreams for Others
"I acknowledge the divinity of every person."

All souls are reflected lights of God's consciousness. All the good we desire for ourselves we should also wish for others. As we do this, we become more cosmic conscious and our recognition of spiritual freedom for others blesses them.

1. What are your fond hopes and dreams for people you know and for every person in this and all worlds?

_____

_____

2. Besides your prayers and good will, what practical things are you doing (or can you do) to assist others in the direction of their highest good?

_____

_____

3. What are your hopes and dreams for Planet Earth, and what are you doing (or can you do) to nurture the environment?

_____

_____

_____

_____

My Personal Affirmation of Realization
"In confidence and faith, I speak the Word of Truth."

It is spiritually helpful to clearly write and intentionally affirm our vision of possibilities for ourselves and others. Write an affirmation, in the present tense, as though it were now fully actualized, that best defines your intuitive certainty of final outcomes of your committed endeavors and unfoldments of God's grace. Then speak it aloud with conviction and realization.

_____

_____

_____

_____

_____

_____

_____

_____

_____

_____

_____

_____

APPENDIX

Our Awakening World

Imagine that in a matter of days, many thousands of men, women, and children representative of the global population were to be contacted and only one question was asked: "What do you think, above all else, the world needs most?" What do you suppose the answers would be?

Some of them would surely be: An end to hunger, economic stability, plenty of resources, permanent peace among groups and nations, absence of race and ethnic prejudice and religious bigotry, more cooperation between people, a more nurturing attitude and behavior toward the environment and more prudent use of its resources— all of which are certainly to be desired.

Many would undoubtedly say: What the world needs most of all, is love. Yes, compassionate caring will be very helpful in enabling us to solve primary problems, especially those directly related to personal interactions and environmental relationships. Knowledge of how to demonstrate love is also needed, for love without ability to intelligently function cannot meet all needs, nor enable us to implement our plans and programs; for good intentions without skillful actions are impotent.

What the world really needs—and is getting—are more intelligent, emotionally mature people who are able to live out of awakened spiritual consciousness, for the best of human efforts cannot accomplish what awakened spiritual consciousness can make possible out of itself.

With awakened spiritual consciousness, we see more

clearly, live with enlightened purpose, and perform all actions with wisdom-guided excellence. More obviously: awakened spiritual consciousness spontaneously results in ordered thinking, appropriate behaviors, and ideal outcomes because of the ruling influence of God's grace in our lives and in world affairs. Our best endeavors, while necessary, cannot do what God's grace can do. But we cannot sit on the sidelines, expecting grace to be operative while we do nothing, for grace is experienced in direct proportion to our responsiveness to it—to the degree that we can allow it to express through and around us.

Our Awakening World: Present Status and Future Conditions

I am writing these words in the first half of the last decade of the 20th century. A few generations from now, readers of this book will be able to determine the accuracy of what is here shared regarding the trend of the times and what I, and many others, presently envision for the planet and its inhabitants. I admit to having knowledge of certain esoteric principles which are not today generally known or understood by many people, but which will henceforth be available to those who care to examine them.

When in possession of higher knowledge, whether acquired or self-revealed, we are in a much improved relationship with planetary circumstances and enabled to see the outer and inner causes of events and conditions. We can then more easily remain soul centered and calm while involved in instrumental changes beyond our personal control, and intentionally implementing spiritual, mental, and physical actions which are in accord with evolutionary trends and purposes.

Even though our sojourn here is but an interlude in our

much longer soul journey in space-time, while we are on Earth it is our abode, as it will be the galactic home of countless billions of souls for many millions of solar years in the future. During our visit here we are in relationship with the planet and the universe, and we are wise to be responsible participants. Disinterested involvement with Nature and unfolding events merely reveals our own spiritual deficiency. Arrogant behavior in relationship to life processes and society is symptomatic of psychological conflict. To be desired, necessary even, is reverence for life and an understanding participation with its processes. It is in this way that we fulfill our obligation to nurture the planet and contribute to the culturing of society. Our own enlightened purposes can then be more efficiently fulfilled and we can be assured of the full support of Nature's laws—being provided with a sufficiency of all things while not depleting the supply of available natural resources.

The last third of the 20th century was remarkable in many ways—and one issue that has been rarely considered before now has been widely acknowledged: the care and preservation of the planet. Astronomy and space exploration provide reports that confirm what biology and geophysics reveal. The planetary actions governing climate, soils, and plants are complex and fragile—and we are dependent upon them. Our behaviors in relationship to planetary systems and the considerable increase in human population provides added impact to natural terrestrial forces. Science-based technologies and industrialization are posing new threats to the environment.

The June 1992 United Nations Conference on Environment and Development in Rio de Janeiro focused world attention on many matters of pressing concern. International media has published much information everyone needs to know and think about. Local air pollution, regional acid rainfall, signs of global warming, and the thinning of the ozone layer testify to the global effects of industrialization. To these conditions we can add solid waste landfills; toxic chemical dumps; the contamination of lakes, groundwater, and streams; soil erosion on all continents; and the impoverishment and destruction of ecosystems invaded by human habitation. All this, and more, is the life-threatening price the world has been paying for the benefits of the 25 percent of the population that lives in industrialized countries—who consume 75 percent of the material wealth and resources.

Wasteful slash and burn practices account for 35 percent of the deforestation in the Amazon region, 50 percent in South and Southeast Asia, and 70 percent in Africa. Water reserves are rapidly diminishing as the population continues to swell. It is population growth that disturbs the stable relation with the forests, land used for agriculture, and water supplies, and the quality of life on Earth within the near future will be related, to a considerable degree, to the size of global population.

At present, food needs can easily be met so long as favorable political circumstances prevail. However, we are realizing that natural resources, for fuel and consumer products, are not inexhaustible and many are being depleted at an alarming rate. New fuel sources will have to be discovered and utilized, materials recycled and waste minimized. Thankfully these matters are already known to us and public and private attention is being focused on them. One of the reasons for the growing population is that people are living longer than before. People in heavily populated regions where natural resources are becoming more scarce are more challenged and will have to adopt new ways of utilizing existing resources or relocate to areas which are more suitable. At present, almost four-fifths of the global population of nearly 7 billion people live in developing regions where living conditions are more precarious. It is estimated that by early in the 21st century four-fifths of all consumer goods will be used by people in these regions of the world.

In regions where economic conditions are more stable, mostly in the northern hemisphere, besides weather, soil, pollution, and resource challenges, another, more subtle problem exists: that of having meaningful purpose. When material want no longer dominates our lives, when we have all we need for comfort and expression, what then? More and more, machines are doing the work formerly done by people. In the United States, for instance, less than 3 percent of the work force is engaged in agriculture and less than 30 percent in the production of consumer goods. Not only has arduous physical toil virtually disappeared in industrially advanced countries, but even light, repetitive work and much mental work has been given over to machines and computers.

Two of the signs of lack of adaptation of the changing circumstances are habitual unemployment and purposelessness. When people have to work for a living they at least have something to look forward to, something to engage their minds and energies. Now social unrest and preoccupation with the isolated self are a central theme of our culture and in other countries where most personal economic problems have a fairly easy solution. Governments and social institutions cannot solve the individual's personal problem of lack of self-identity and of having a sense of meaningful purpose in life—this has to come from within the person.

Shorter and fewer working days for the employed and years of prolonged education and earlier retirement are the principle products of automated production methods. More young people are going beyond high school to college and more older ones are taking earlier retirement. What are we to do with our extra free time, now that we no longer have to work long hours to earn enough money to take care of our needs and we live longer after retirement? The obvious solution is to become purposefully involved in social service, become educated and cultured, and to improve our knowledge of how to live. The cultivation of awakened spiritual consciousness should definitely be included in our total program, for it is precisely the lack of interest in spiritual growth that is at the root of the problem of psychological unrest which results in addictive behaviors, immoral and unethical actions, crimes of various kinds, and social conflicts. Most people would be much more successful and healthier if they were mentally and emotionally at peace with themselves, if they would allow themselves time to devote to honest self-analysis and spiritual growth. They would then find it to be easy and natural to help others less fortunate and to treat the environment with the respect and kindness it needs. Poverty, want, political conflicts, and wars between groups and nations would be absent from the world scene.

We are moving toward a Global Community consciousness. Regional and national boundaries, cultural traditions, and societal modes which have value to groups will persist, while a prevailing sense of Human Family will be the basis of compassionate cooperation. Ours is not a very large planet. A commercial jet airplane can fly around it in less than two days. Radio, television, telephone, and computer link-ups enable us to communicate with each other almost anywhere in the world in a matter of seconds. What happened this morning in a remote region of a distant country is a broadcast news item by noon, with complete global coverage by early evening.

There will always be differences between people because of their unique states of consciousness, psychological states, and personal preferences. But our common divinity can be acknowledged and our basic, essential freedoms of expression honored and protected. Individuals who persist in argumentative confrontation, who are demonstrative in expressing their prejudiced, self-serving views, will have no voice in the New Era now dawning. Their voices will be muted and their actions rendered ineffectual against the tides of transformational changes being manifested by the irresistible currents of evolution.

An extended era of almost complete global enlightenment will not immediately unfold, for mass spiritual awakening can only occur in the field of relative time. But we are moving ever more rapidly in the direction of a true Golden Age, as present trends indicate and some prescient persons predict. The assurance of philosopher-seers who claim to have special knowledge and intuitive insight is that, despite the many obvious challenges before us, a marvelous future is now unfolding on the screen of space-time and future generations will enjoy unprecedented good fortune and highly developed soul capacities.

Historical records and oral traditions provide us with some knowledge of the past. We now know that civilizations rise and fall in sequential cycles, the causes of which are attributable to a variety of circumstances. Earth changes, due to the shifting of the planet's crust, volcanic activity, occasional large meteorite impacts, periodic Ice Ages, dramatic weather and climate changes, and the benevolent or destructive behaviors of humankind, have their effects. There is little we can do about some of the natural, cataclysmic processes except to adapt to changing conditions. But there are many things we can do to nurture the planet and live in harmony with its actions and the forces which express through and around it. And there is much we can do to cultivate awakened spiritual consciousness, our own and that of others, which will enable us to more wisely proceed and prevail.

There are also other, little known but actively involved, factors which have influence. One is the unfolding destiny of souls working out their salvation in relationship to the planet; the other is the effects of cosmic forces upon our mental faculties. An understanding of these factors is somewhat determined by our ability to intellectually and intuitively comprehend their existence and modes of action.

Souls incarnate when and where conditions are best suited to their psychological and spiritual needs. When large numbers of souls with similar states of consciousness inhabit the Earth, their states of consciousness and behaviors tend to be dominant. Societal conditions then reflect their actions.

More influential than collective consciousness, however, are the cosmic forces which somewhat influence our subtle, mental perceptual faculties. I am aware of the fact that some spiritual aspirants prefer to believe themselves to be impervious to external influences and do not like to think about such possibilities. However, I feel it to be useful for us to at least fairly examine what some wise persons have to say about cosmic forces and their actions and influences.

The theory of electric time-cycles set forth here was first published in our present era in 1894 by my guru's guru, Sri Yukteswar, in India. Having researched Vedic scriptures and available astronomical evidence, Sri Yukteswar discovered that quickening, or slowing and declining, of intellectual and spiritual capacities is directly related to our solar system's proximity to the source of creative power or cosmic magnetism at the galactic center.

From a study of astronomy we learn that moons revolve around their planets, planets turning on their axis revolve around the sun; and the sun, with its planets, revolves around its dual in about 24,000 years of solar time. When the sun in its movement begins to approach the source of creative power in the galaxy, mankind's intellectual and intuitive powers become more developed, increasing powers of perception. When the sun in its movement moves away from the source of creative power in the galaxy, mankind's intellectual and intuitive powers become somewhat obscured, diminishing powers of perception and creativity.

The following brief overview of this theory of electric time-cycles will reveal that the present world era is that of the second ascending cycle, during which more rapid unfoldment of knowledge is occurring. We are, therefore, in a time-cycle which is advantageous for higher learning and more rapid spiritual growth.

There are two 12,000 year electric time-cycles comprising each 24,000 total cycle: one which occurs as the sun moves toward the central seat of universal magnetism, and one which occurs as the sun moves away from it. When the sun is at its farthest point from the galactic power center and the intellectual powers of the majority of people on Earth are diminished, a Dark Age era prevails, the duration of which is 2400 years or two segments of 1200 years each. The last Dark Age ended about 1700 A.D. and we have been moving into the ascending cycle of 2400 years which follows it, hence the rapid intellectual awakening during the past 300 years and more recent, dramatic intellectual attainments and scientific discoveries.

A little over two thousand years from now (around 4011) we will be moving into the third ascending segment of the cycle which will be a Mental Age, during which the majority of people on the planet will have highly developed intellectual powers and be able to comprehend the existence of divine magnetism and other cosmic forces which nourish creation.

Then will follow, beginning around 7700, a true era of enlightenment or Golden Age of Truth comprehension.

Most people on Earth will then be able to understand the nature and reality of God and spontaneously live in harmony with each other and the universe. Their inner realization and outer demeanor will be like that of persons whom we today consider to be saints or sages.

Many students of metaphysics and Eastern philosophical systems are of the mistaken opinion that we are currently still in a Dark Age cycle. The reason for this is because until recently very few writers knew of the theory of electric time-cycles explained here. A major fault was committed during the descent of the last Dark Age around 700 B.C. when astronomers of that time, not wanting to inform the public about the coming decline in their fortunes, altered the records to try to show that the previous higher Age would persist. With the coming of the Dark Age there were no discerning astronomers available to note the error. When it was finally discovered near the end of the descending Dark Age cycle, the reason for the wrong information was not known. Referring to the calculations of ancient seers, it was found that the Dark Age cycle was of a duration of 1200 years. Since Dark Age conditions prevailed, it was assumed that these were not ordinary solar years of 365 days but were "years of the gods," each of which consisted of 12 such months of 30 days, each day calculated as being equal to one solar year of our Earth. They thus wrongly determined that the Dark Age cycle would extend to 432,000 Earth years, a faulty conclusion that has been proclaimed by some people for centuries.

I have occasionally pointed out this error to teachers who have been vocal in their support of the much longer Dark Age theory. Some have grasped the facts of the matter immediately. Others have said that it makes sense but is not the "traditional" belief and they would rather not go against prevailing attitudes. In these pages I am glad to once again clarify the issue for the benefit of readers large-minded and discerning enough to comprehend and appreciate it.

Understanding which is common knowledge during the higher time-cycles is not always so easily experienced during lower ones. In our current ascending Age of Awakening, Dark Age influences and attitudes yet prevail because humanity is only now beginning to wake up. It is often easier to pretend to be moral and ethical than it is to actually embody these virtues because of them being spontaneous manifestations of our soul qualities. It is more likely that the average spiritual aspirant or religious devotee will be satisfied to imitate practices and rituals instead of "living the life" to the fullest extent possible in order to actualize divine capacities. Many thus make a pretense of the spiritual path, a mock attempt at appearing to be holy, to somewhat placate and dull their conscience while continuing in their self-satisfied ways. Their problems are: egoism, due to strong identification with mind and matter which results in a false sense of individual existence apart from God; delusion, because of egoism, which results in restricted awareness and difficulty in knowing truth from untruth; and mental perversity, the self-defeating habit of distorting valid knowledge to serve self-centered purposes. All of these problems can be quickly solved by sincere spiritual endeavor and God's grace if one is surrendered to the enlightenment process.

How to Live as An Enlightened
Person Regardless of the Times
and Changing Circumstances

The more Self-realized and God-conscious we are, the less are we influenced by cosmic forces and environmental circumstances. The ideal is to experience conditions which reflect enlightened states of consciousness at all times. This is accomplished by surrendered devotion to God, intentional spiritual practice, the awakening of innate intelligence, and practical application of known principles. To do these things we have to be willing to awaken from all illusions and fully come to terms with our spiritual reality. We are then removed from the influences which determine the lives of spiritually unawake persons. We can relate to all people with love and good will, while maintaining our own integrity and enlightened understanding. This is what it means to be in the world but not of it; to overcome the world's influences while embodied and while continuing to render useful service.

By adopting a personal life style which is fully supportive of your enlightened purposes and spiritual growth, you will overcome all destructive tendencies and neutralize the effects of past imprudent actions. You will become mentally and physically healthy, successful in ventures, understandingly appreciative of the gift of life, and will more rapidly awaken to higher levels of consciousness until full God-realization is stable. With expanded states of awareness you will comprehend higher realities and know all things. Your enlightened consciousness and flows of creative forces through your body and mind will cleanse body and mind of all impurities. Your nervous system will be refined, enabled to process God-conscious states during your routine waking and sleeping hours. You will have nothing more for which to strive, nothing more to attain, nothing more to do except dispassionately perform your wisdom-guided service for the sake of others and to assist the evolution of the world.

Accept the ways of the universe. Accept God's redeeming grace. Acknowledge all souls as being as divine as your Self and let your life be an example after which they might model their own. Many spiritual lights have come into the world through the Ages, and they continue to come, to fulfill their destiny and infuse planetary consciousness with divine impulses. Honor them, while being not forgetful to honor your own Selfhood, your own divinity. Learn of them while you are yet growing in grace and truth, remembering that you must become as they are. The seeker of knowledge must become a knower. The disciple must become a spiritual master. The one who endeavors must awaken to realize that God alone is the doer. The free soul must be a servant of God. These are some things to remember.

ROY EUGENE DAVIS is the spiritual director of the Center for Spiritual Awareness and a world-traveled teacher of meditation and spiritual growth processes.

Born in a farming community in northern Ohio (1931) he began his personal quest for higher understanding while in high school. He met his guru, Paramahansa Yogananda, in Los Angeles, California, in 1949 and devoted the next four years to intensive study and spiritual practices as a member of the Self-Realization Fellowship monastic community. He was ordained by Yoganandaji in 1951 and served (1952-53) as minister of the SRF Branch Center in Phoenix, Arizona. Then followed two years in the U.S. Army Medical Corps before beginning his present ministry.

Mr. Davis has taught in over 100 U.S. cities, Canada, Brazil, England, Europe, and West Africa, and has visited India several times. He is the author of several books, some of which are published in six languages, publisher of *Truth Journal* magazine, and writes a series of monthly lesson guides for students and truth seekers of many countries. He is also a frequent guest speaker and meditation seminar leader for New Thought churches and at yoga retreats and holistic wellness conferences.

CENTER FOR SPIRITUAL AWARENESS

With international headquarters and retreat center on an eleven acre, wooded site in the mountains of northeast Georgia, the Center for Spiritual Awareness serves all who sincerely desire to learn to live a God-centered life. While honoring all authentic enlightenment traditions and modes of religious worship, the emphasis is upon spiritual growth and demonstrated, self-responsible living.

Meditation retreats are offered from spring to autumn, to which many hundreds of persons come annually from all parts of North America and other countries. Facilities include the administration building, private meditation temple, library, main meeting hall, and four comfortable guest houses. Vegetarian meals are served during retreats. Retreat themes include yoga philosophy and practice, meditation, wellness regimens, and workshops to encourage functional living. Occasional guest presenters offer seminars featuring Ayurveda and Sanskrit learning. Programs for children are scheduled each summer.

CSA Press is the literature department of Center for Spiritual Awareness and maintains an active publishing program which includes books, magazines, printed lessons, and audio and video presentations.

Branch meditation centers are located in several U.S. cities, Canada, Europe, and West Africa.

Free information literature and a book list
will be sent anywhere in the world upon request.

Center for Spiritual Awareness
Lake Rabun Road, Post Office Box 7
Lakemont, Georgia 30552
U.S.A.

Telephone (706) 782-4723
Fax   (706) 782-4560

Share a copy of *The Book of Life* with others whom you know to be interested in spiritual growth.

Obtain copies from your book seller or direct from the publisher. If ordering from CSA Press, include $4.95 for the book and $1.50 postage in the United States. Other countries: add $2.00 for surface mail to the cost of the book or $4.00 for airmail.

For larger quantities contact the publisher for discount prices and cost of shipping estimate.

Book sellers, order at usual trade terms.

CSA PRESS, Publishers
Post Office Box 7
Lakemont, Georgia 30552
U.S.A.

Telephone (706) 782-4723